Other Books by Ace Collins

Turn Your Radio On: The Stories Behind Gospel Music's All-Time Greatest Songs

Stories Behind the Best-Loved Songs of Christmas

★ STORIES BEHIND THE HYMNS THAT INSPIRE AMERICA ★

SONGS THAT UNITE OUR NATION

ACE COLLINS

ILLUSTRATIONS BY CLINT HANSEN

Zondervan

Grand Rapids, Michigan 49530 USA

We want to hear from you. Please send your comments about this book to us in care of zreview@zondervan.com. Thank you.

Zondervan

Grand Rapids, Michigan 49530 USA
www.zondervan.com

Zondervan

Stories Behind the Hymns That Inspire America
Copyright © 2003 by Andrew Collins

Requests for information should be addressed to:

Zondervan, *Grand Rapids, Michigan 49530*

ISBN 0-310-24879-5

Illustrations by Clint Hansen
Interior design by Todd Sprague

Printed in the United States of America

To those men and women
who have gone all over the world
entertaining American troops
through the programs and tours
sponsored by the USO

CONTENTS

INTRODUCTION

The songs in this book were either written about the United States, have made an important contribution during this country's most historic times, or have inspired Americans during moments of great tribulation. The stories behind these twenty-five songs, some of them actually composed in other countries, reflect the blessings of living in a free nation where liberty is available to all.

Though the U.S. government has traditionally drawn a line between church and state—and as time has proven, this line has actually enhanced the work and growth of the church—faith has always played a part in the history of America. Since the days when the first Europeans landed on the shores of the New World, religion has been one of the primary forces that has inspired those who have come here to embrace this nation with such vigor and passion.

Each of the songs in this book combines America and Christianity in a way that reflects the impact of country and faith on the timeline of history. These songs of faith have provided inspiration, recorded history, taken the message of freedom and faith across this nation and beyond, delivered comfort, healed broken spirits, righted wrongs, and reminded Americans of the blessings to be found in this unique democracy. Each song stands alone in power and majesty, but each also serves as a tool to bring people together. Some of these hymns wrap themselves in the red, white, and blue, while others reflect America in a more subtle way. Yet each is very special to this country, its story, and its people.

In this nation even one voice can have a lasting impact. The writers of these songs prove this fact and provide each citizen with a model that stands not only for the power of faith but also for the reality of the American Dream. The next time you sing one of these songs that have inspired America, remember that it was born when God touched one person in a very special way and that person responded to his touch. In other words, thanks to the freedom found in this land of liberty, you have the same power to impact America and share your faith as did those whose stories are told in these pages.

God bless you, and God bless America!

AMAZING GRACE

*I*f America were to have a national Christian hymn, many would argue that it would have to be "Amazing Grace." Because of its roots and the miraculous turnaround found in its message, "Amazing Grace" is a song that reflects both the good and the bad found in America's past, present, and future, as well as on the road to individual salvation.

This inspirational standard, written, ironically, by an Englishman, was born not from an experience of love but from a sordid tale of human exploitation. So while much of what is both human and divine can be seen in John Newton's short verses, to fully appreciate the hymn one must know the story behind it and discover the verse that has now been deleted from the song.

John Newton was born in London, England, on August 4, 1725. Though he was not poor, Newton did not have a wonderful or secure home life. His father was a hardened sailor, the owner of a trade ship that sailed the Mediterranean. The elder Newton was often gone for months at a time, leaving the boy alone with his mother. Mrs. Newton was a loving Christian woman, a devoted parent who took a vital interest in her son, but she was also chronically ill and physically weak. Because of his mother's frailty, John literally had the run of the house from the time he could walk. The energetic child was in constant trouble, often missed school, and was usually at the center of neighborhood pranks. After his mother died when he was only seven, his one hope for a normal life ended. He dropped out of school, all but living on the streets. Four years later, at the age of eleven, John followed in his father's footsteps and became a cabin boy on a ship. It was probably the only thing that kept him out of juvenile prison, but it didn't keep him out of trouble.

Even as a teenager, Newton was hard drinking and ill-tempered. Law officers in the port towns called the youth vicious, brutal, and fearless. His public brawls were legendary. When he wasn't in jail, he could often be found in a ship's brig. Newton even scared veteran sailors with his unpredictable and violent behavior. By the time he was twenty, he had lived enough adventures to fill the lives of four men, spilled more blood than most career soldiers, and consumed enough alcohol to stock London's largest pub. He later described himself as a godless monster, and few who knew him during his youth would have disagreed.

His attitude and illegal exploits finally drove him out of Europe to Sierra Leone, on the west coast of Africa. There Newton discovered a band of men who were as wild and depraved as he. For the next few years this group was responsible for untold suffering and death. Newton and his shipmates sought out tribal chiefs and traded guns, spices, liquor, and clothes for strong young native men and women. This innocent human cargo was then loaded aboard tiny ships and transported across the Atlantic to the New World. Of the more than six hundred people who were literally chained shoulder to shoulder in each ship's hold, between 20 and 40 percent died on the journey. Those who somehow

Amazing grace! how sweet
   the sound,
That saved a wretch like me!
I once was lost, but now am
   found,
Was blind, but now I see.

'Twas grace that taught my
   heart to fear,
And grace my fears relieved;
How precious did that grace
   appear
The hour I first believed!

Through many dangers, toils
   and snares,
I have already come;
'Tis grace hath brought me
   safe thus far,
And grace will lead me
   home.

The Lord has promised good
   to me,
His Word my hope secures;

He will my Shield and
   Portion be,
As long as life endures.

Yea, when this flesh and
   heart shall fail,
And mortal life shall cease,
I shall possess, within the
   veil,
A life of joy and peace.

The earth shall soon dissolve
   like snow,
The sun forbear to shine;
But God, Who called me
   here below,
Shall be forever mine.

When we've been there ten
   thousand years,
Bright shining as the sun,
We've no less days to sing
   God's praise
Than when we first begun.

survived were then sold at auctions, and Newton and his shipmates shared the bounty. In most ports, pirates were considered more respectable and honorable than slavers; thus, Newton was considered one of the lowest of the men who sailed the seas.

John Newton's decadent life was fueled by America's demand for slaves. Strangely, many of the men who bought Newton's cargo were Christians who found no moral dilemma in their actions. Some slave owners were even ministers. The moral indifference of many in the church just made it easier for Newton to help engineer a system that reflected the very worst of humanity. Like millions of others, he felt no regret and no shame. In the slave trade, black human beings were just soulless products to use and dispose of. As Newton tossed dead men and women overboard or watched others being sold on auction blocks, he could only say, "So be it."

The time spent crossing the Atlantic offered sailors an opportunity to play cards, swap stories, or read. In 1758 twenty-three-year-old Newton was studying a book called *The Imitation of Christ*. By now this veteran of several slave runs could easily tune out the moans and screams of the chained cargo. He had also grown used to the smell of the human waste, disease, and death that came from the cargo hold. Nothing really bothered him, not even a fellow crew-man dragging a dead body up on the deck and heaving it overboard.

On this calm day as Newton read, he forgot about the world around him. He grew so lost in the pages of his book that he even failed to note the storm that had quickly gathered in the west. Only when wild winds began to jostle the

ship's masts and pelting rain hit the deck did the
sailor turn his attention from Thomas A. Kempis's *The Imitation of Christ* to his duties. By then it appeared to be too late.

The storm that suddenly struck the slave ship that day
was the worst Newton had ever experienced. As the ship was
tossed about like a leaf in the wind, rolling from side to side,
the veteran of scores of storms sensed that this time he was
not going to survive. He felt sure the ship was going to be
crushed and he would be tossed into an unforgiving sea with
no hope of rescue. While others cried, cursed, and begged,
Newton thought back on his own
miserable life. As the Atlantic
churned back and forth
across the decks, the
sailor concluded that the
only person he had ever
known who really loved
him was his mother. He
also realized she would be
heartbroken if she knew
what he had become. Feeling a
need to try to seek some kind of redemption before it was too
late, Newton fell to his knees, clinging to a rope, and began
to pray. He pleaded with the Lord to save him. The sailor
promised that if God would give him a second chance at life,
then Newton would become a moral man.

In a matter of minutes the storm abated and roared off to
the east. Miraculously, not one person lost his life that day,
and the mildly damaged ship was able to complete its journey and deliver its cargo. Yet for the first time, when Newton

was given his cut of the profits, he did not seek out a bar to celebrate. Instead, the man who had felt the touch of God's saving hand returned to his ship and read the Bible.

Within two years of the storm, John Newton became the captain of a slave ship. He oversaw his cargo from the capturing and chaining of young African natives to the delivering to auction blocks of those who lived through the ocean crossing. Yet as he watched his men carry out these operations, he could no longer say, "So be it." With Christ in his heart, the immorality of his acts began to nag at Newton's soul. Unable to mesh his Christian convictions with his duties as a slave trade captain, Newton resigned, returned to England, and sought a way to serve Christ. Under the guidance of Charles Wesley, the famous father of the Methodist movement, the former hardened sailor and slave trader became a preacher.

In 1779, two decades after he was literally and spiritually saved, Newton was pastoring a church in Olney, England. One Sunday morning he delivered a message on the grace of Jesus. From the pulpit the now respected moral voice and beloved community leader spoke of his life at sea. He freely admitted his past sins and told his congregation how the Lord had come to him during a violent storm. He finished his message by singing an autobiographical song that began with this touching but now forgotten verse.

> *In evil long I took delight,*
> *Unawed by shame or fear,*
> *Till a new object struck my sight,*
> *And stopped my wild career.*

Newton's "Amazing Grace" may have been composed for a single sermon, but it quickly made its way into songbooks. The hymn was published the same year it was written, and it was quickly brought to the United States. In America, Newton's verses were matched to a number of different tunes, but it was a folk song called both "Kentucky Harmony" and "Virginia Harmony" that became the vehicle that took the message across the new frontier and then back to England. Ironically, "Amazing Grace" first gained wide acceptance in the American South. Little did those in slave states realize that the song had been inspired by a man's realization of the immorality of the very thing that was sustaining many of their livelihoods. By the start of the Civil War, after the familiar final verse was added by an unknown American, "Amazing Grace" was one of the best-known Christian songs in the world. It was also so associated with the United States and the early missionary movement from this country that most believed it to be the product of an American author.

Popular black gospel singers such as W. M. Nic and Roberta Martin made the English song a spiritual anchor in African-American music circles in the early 1900s. The song was popular with troops in both World War I and World War II and was often used at navy funerals at sea and at army and marine battlefront memorials. Later, popular musicians such as Hank Williams and Elvis Presley sang "Amazing Grace" at many of their concerts. It was also a standard in almost every Christian songbook. Yet it wasn't until 1971 that the song climbed out of the nation's hymnbooks and into the mainstream.

Folk-rock songstress Judy Collins probably recorded "Amazing Grace" as much as an act of protest as she did as a symbol of faith. With the divisions caused by the Vietnam War, American cultural clashes, government scandals, and fights for racial equality, Collins's version of "Amazing Grace" became a mirror that reflected the wrongs that seemed to be taking over the nation. Yet as the public voted the old hymn to the top position on the rock charts, the message was transformed and "Amazing Grace" came to mean something else altogether. Americans might have deserted God, but he had not deserted any of those who had seemingly fallen so far from him. In the midst of all the chaos, "Amazing Grace" became a part of a revival movement in which millions again found faith in God and rediscovered faith in their own country at the same time. In the early seventies, whenever the old hymn was played on the radio or sung in public it seemed to reflect the fact that no matter how bad things were, no matter how far individuals and the nation had sunk, even in these stormy historic times there was still the opportunity to ask God for a second chance.

In the past three decades "Amazing Grace" has become almost as much an American icon as the flag, and in some ways these two national symbols represent many of the same concepts and ideals. America is a place where faith seems to surface even in the worst of times, where past mistakes are admitted and wrongs are slowly righted, and where the lost are usually found. John Newton did not have America or Americans in mind when he wrote his testimony into a song, yet at the age of eighty-two he said something that all Christians in this country and around the world can cling to in times of both triumph and trial: "My memory is nearly gone, but I remember two things, that I am a great sinner, and that Christ is a great Savior."

John Newton's "Amazing Grace" is a road map showing how to seek forgiveness and then explaining what that forgiveness can mean to the past, present, and future of all who accept Jesus as Lord. Perhaps that is why this hymn has come to mean so much to Americans and why, as long as it does mean so much, the United States still has a chance to find its moral voice and lead the world with grace, compassion, and charity.

AMERICA, THE BEAUTIFUL

When Samuel Ward was a boy in Newark, New Jersey, in the 1850s, there was no indication the gifted child would have much impact on the world. Though Ward's ancestors were founders of Newark and heroes of the Revolutionary War, the city and the nation had grown a great deal since then. Ward could not perceive how he would escape a humdrum life and rise to prominence even in his own neighborhood, much less in the nation. So rather than fortune or fame, his one real wish in life was to somehow make a living through what he loved the most—music. Ward did not know that this choice would not only bring him great joy but ultimately would make a greater impact on the United States than anything ever accomplished by those from his illustrious family tree.

At the age of six, when Ward began to play the accordion, it was just a small indication of what was to come. By the time he was a teenager he was teaching piano lessons to help support his family. He moved to New York and became a professional church organist at sixteen. Ward was at the right place at the right time doing the right thing when, in the days after the Civil War, band music exploded onto the national scene. Sensing the nation's growing interest in all things musical, the young man opened a store in which he taught piano and sold everything from instruments to sheet music. By the age of thirty, he was married, had a family of four daughters,

and was considered a successful businessman.
Ward was now so financially secure he even took vacations
in Europe.

By 1890 Ward had formed his own male vocal group.
Under his leadership the Orpheus Society became one of
New York's best-known choirs. Ward didn't just direct the
group, he also wrote and arranged much of their music.
Though many around him were now calling the clean-cut,
distinguished-looking man a genius, the businessman
turned choirmaster still seemed content to be known as
just a friend, husband, and father. By all accounts, even
when things were at their best, Ward simply took one day
at a time, finding a way to enjoy each of them as they
came. This desire to relish the moment and squeeze the
most out of life led him to create the musical foundation for
one of America's most loved patriotic hymns.

Coney Island was hardly an awe-inspiring place. The
amusement park was like a carnival gone wild. Huge in
scope, the playground of New York was a place to have fun
and spend money. Part circus and part medieval fair, with
its rides, sideshows, food plazas, and beach, Coney Island
was American capitalism and consumption in all its glory.
Most patrons left the Island tired and broke. Yet the deeply
religious Ward seemed to find God's hand everywhere he
went. He could see the Lord in a child's smile, a mother's
hug, or the crashing of an ocean wave. With this kind of
attitude it is hardly surprising that the music store owner
left the park with more energy and in better spirits than
most around him. It was as if the day had just begun and
he had a great deal more to look forward to.

As the paddle-wheel steamship pushed through the bay toward his home, and most of those on board found a chair and rested their worn-out bodies, the energetic Ward took in the sites from the deck, visited with the crew, and listened to two musicians play a tune he had never heard. After they had concluded their performance, Ward began to hum a new melody based on the one the men had just played. With no paper to write down the notes, Ward convinced a friend to let him use the man's removable shirt cuff. Samuel quickly jotted down his musical lines, then stuffed the cuff into his pocket. The next day Ward set his tune to the lyrics of an old hymn, "O Mother Dear, Jerusalem." He called his new arrangement "Materna."

The hymn was first published in the *Parish Choir*, a religious music periodical. From there it found its way into several hymnals. While his friends were deeply impressed with what Ward had accomplished, he didn't fully grasp the beauty of his work until he happened to hear a children's choir singing "O Mother Dear, Jerusalem" with his new tune. Listening to innocent voices move through something he had written brought the man to tears.

Samuel Ward composed several other hymns before his death in 1903. Yet thanks to a children's choir, it was the tune that came to him after a trip to Coney Island that remained his favorite. Little did he know it would also become his legacy.

In 1893 thirty-three-year-old Katherine Bates was a teacher at Wellesley College in Boston. A graduate of the school and the daughter of a minister, Bates had already established herself as one of the top English teachers at the

O beautiful for spacious skies,
For amber waves of grain,
For purple mountain majesties
Above the fruited plain!
America! America!
God shed his grace on thee,
And crown thy good with
    brotherhood
From sea to shining sea!

O beautiful for pilgrim feet,
Whose stern impassioned
    stress
A thoroughfare of freedom
    beat
Across the wilderness!
America! America!
God mend thine every flaw,
Confirm thy soul in self-
    control,
Thy liberty in law!

O beautiful for heroes proved
In liberating strife,
Who more than self their
    country loved,
And mercy more than life!
America! America!
May God thy gold refine,
Till all success be nobleness,
And every gain divine!

O beautiful for patriot dream
That sees beyond the years
Thine alabaster cities gleam,
Undimmed by human tears!
America! America!
God shed his grace on thee,
And crown thy good with
    brotherhood
From sea to shining sea!

prestigious institution when she was asked to go west and teach a summer course at Colorado College in Colorado Springs. Though most single women would not have had the courage to undertake such an adventure, Bates possessed a pioneer's heart. So, naturally, she didn't want to just read about America's rugged frontier; she wanted to see it with her own eyes.

On her way to Colorado, Bates was treated to two thrills that few Americans of that era could claim. She spent a day observing the power and majesty of Niagara Falls and then stopped and toured the huge World's Columbian Exposition in Chicago. This fair, celebrating Columbus's discovery of America, introduced the ice-cream cone, the hot dog, and the Ferris wheel to the world. The fun-loving child in Bates relished every one of those uniquely American inventions, as well as all the rides and the exhibits. But the deeply spiritual woman in Katherine was probably most moved when a choir of ten thousand voices sang "My Country, 'Tis of Thee" as fireworks lit up the night sky. Between the natural wonder of Niagara Falls and the man-made spectacle of the fair in the Windy City, the teacher had experienced a lifetime of delights even before she arrived in Colorado.

Bates's reputation as a master educator probably meant that her students at that summer session were blessed beyond measure. Yet history does not record that any of the young people studying under Bates were actually motivated to follow in the woman's footsteps. While the days spent in the classroom did not dramatically alter the teacher or her students, what happened that July would impact the nation in a way no one could have predicted.

On July 22, 1893, Katherine Bates pulled her short, stout frame onto a mule-drawn wagon. Along with a number of other tourists, she was going on a ride to the top of Pikes Peak. It would take hours for this band to make it up the 14,110-foot mountain, but Bates didn't care. With her spirit of adventure, she relished the opportunity to see not just the mighty vistas that jumped out as the party moved higher and higher up, but she was also thrilled by the opportunity to spy every new flower, tree, bird, and animal that appeared along the way. When she finally got to the top, her breath was taken away.

From a point near the summit, the teacher looked out into a clear sky. Beneath this canopy of blue she saw snow-capped mountains, flat wheat fields that fed a nation, tiny towns, large rivers, and roads that seemed to disappear over the edge of the world. Only a few weeks before, she had believed nothing could move her spirit as had Niagara Falls, but now she realized the view from Pikes Peak was like having heaven come to earth. For a second she must have wondered if this was how God saw the world. Bates later described the view in a letter to a friend: "All the wonder of America seemed displayed there, with the sea-like expanse."

As a child Bates had learned to always carry a notebook and pencil wherever she went, so for twenty-five years she had recorded her thoughts and inspiration in a series of notebooks. As she sat near the top of Pikes Peak, she picked up her notebook and began to write as phrases flew into her mind and almost magically appeared on the paper. The words came so quickly she didn't even feel she was composing a poem. Bates did not consider that what she had written would have any lasting impact in her own life, much less anyone else's. She only wanted to jot down what she observed so she could more accurately share this moment with her friends and family back home.

Several weeks later, after she had returned to Wellesley, Bates picked up the notebook in an effort to recall the moment when she had looked down at the world from the top of Pikes Peak. Yet what she read did not initially impress her. As she would tell others, the words simply didn't measure up to what she had witnessed. Nevertheless, she rewrote her observations and even sent the finished piece to a magazine publisher for consideration. She probably expected to receive a rejection notice, but instead was shocked when the *Congregationalist* opted to use her "America, the Beautiful" in its July 4, 1895, issue.

At this time most magazines published poetry, but rarely did any of these poems make much more than a minor splash with the general public. "America, the Beautiful" was one of the exceptions. Hundreds of subscribers wrote in to the publication praising Bates's work. One man, a musician named Silas Pratt, even sent the *Congregationalist* a melody he had written to go with the poem. This first tune was just the beginning.

Over the course of the next few years, "America, the Beautiful" was reprinted by magazines and newspapers in every corner of the United States. The poem inspired more musicians with each new publication. By 1900 at least seventy-five different tunes were married to Bates's poem. Some were good, most were bad, and few actually seemed to fit well with the written verses. None of these works had any staying power. For the time being, Bates's poem seemed to be most powerful when it was read rather than sung.

In 1904 a Baptist preacher named Clarence A. Barbour decided that no popular or folk tune lyrics could ever match the brilliance of "America, the Beautiful." Barbour believed Bates's verses were so spiritual that they could be mated only to music that had been inspired, not just composed. The preacher turned to his library of Christian songbooks to find an existing melody to match Bates's words. After hours of searching he discovered Samuel Ward's "Materna." Barbour instantly realized he had discovered the soul mate to Bates's poem. It was if they had been written at the same time and inspired by the same vision.

This marriage of music and words made its debut later that year at Boston's Lake Avenue Baptist Church. When it was sung that day it was obvious that what Bates had begun on Pikes Peak was now finished. Yet it would not be until 1910, when Barbour put this version of "America, the Beautiful" into his best-selling *Fellowship Hymns*, that Ward's tune displaced all the others that had been previously used with Bates's now famous poem.

Samuel Ward died a year before his melody completed the work begun by Katherine Bates at Pikes Peak. The musician would have no doubt been shocked to know that something he wrote could so move a nation during peace and war. Meanwhile, Katherine Bates did not die until 1929, so she lived long enough to realize that her poem, "America, the Beautiful," had become the nation's best-loved patriotic hymn. While it is well known that Bates did revel in the notoriety her words brought to her, few realize the woman did not make a single claim for song royalties during her life. Likewise, Ward's family asked for no payment for the use of the tune. Bates and the Wards felt this song had been inspired by God. In their minds it was his hand that had directed the two separate pens working from two different points of view. They always believed it was the Lord who brought the two elements together to make "America, the Beautiful" complete. In other words, the song was and is God's gift to America.

Author's note: There has probably been more written about "America, the Beautiful" than any other song, with the possible exception of "Silent Night." This chapter touches on only the high points of this wonderful American hymn's history. To find out the complete story, please read Lynn Sherr's book, *America, the Beautiful,* published by Public Affairs Books in 2001. In this eloquently written work, the esteemed ABC television reporter presents a story that is as uplifting as is the song. Sherr's research breaks new ground, and she wonderfully entertains as she informs.

AN AMERICAN TRILOGY

One of the most beautiful facets of Christian faith is forgiveness. Forgiveness brings healing. Forgiveness is the essence of salvation and paves the way for the peace that can be a part of every believer's life. Yet forgiveness is one part of faith that many find very hard to put into practice. Therefore old wounds often continue to fester and old hates and fears continue to push prejudice into the hearts, minds, and actions of those who call themselves Christians.

On a cool night in Los Angeles in the late 1960s, Mickey Newbury, a Texas-born songwriter, experienced a dramatic moment of inspiration that became a tool of healing for a wound that had divided this nation for more than a century. Newbury's "An American Trilogy" is therefore more than a song of praise; it is a musical portrait of this country at its spiritual worst and its spiritual best.

Mickey Newbury was born on the eve of World War II. In his teens he landed a recording contract as a rock-and-roll singer. Yet the young man with the gentle soul was not your typical rebel without a cause. He was a thinker—a spiritual person who saw a constant connection with the world and its maker. Naturally his music took on his uniquely spiritual views. So during a time when most popular songs dealt with the traumas of going steady or the challenges of drag racing, Newbury's early work didn't spend much time on radio playlists.

A stint in the air force took the young man to England, where he met another unknown enlisted man destined for fame, Kris Kristofferson. The two aspiring musicians spent their spare hours playing guitar, writing songs, and discussing subjects that included both men's quest to find God's hand in their work. Upon being discharged, both Mickey and Kris migrated to Nashville seeking a career in the music business. Kristofferson found fame first, but Newbury was not far behind. He penned a number of hits such as "Why You Been Gone So Long," "Sweet Memories," "She Even Woke Me Up to Say Good-bye," "How I Love Them Old Songs," and "Just Dropped In (To See What Condition My Condition Is In)." His compositions for Andy Williams, Eddy Arnold, Willie Nelson, Solomon Burke, and Kenny Rogers topped the charts. In a city awash with great talent, Newbury was recognized as one of the very best of Nashville's new generation of tunesmiths.

Newbury's work as a writer and his spiritual view of the world made him a hot nightclub act in the turbulent sixties and seventies. The songwriter did more than touch people's hearts; he also forced their brains into action. In a world gone mad with fear and distrust, in a nation divided by race, an unpopular war, and a laundry list of social issues, Newbury's introspective and spiritual compositions were not just listened to, they were talked about. Many even looked to the man's lyrics for answers to the day's troubling problems.

It was when Mickey was booked into New York City's famous Bitter End nightclub in the late sixties that events were set into motion that brought forth his most controversial and spiritual work. This song, written and arranged extemporaneously during his live performance, was born

when the manager of the Bitter End demanded that Newbury not sing a specific song of the old South.

"The manager told me I couldn't sing the song 'Dixie,'" Newbury recalled. "He said his crowd would take offense at that kind of racist song."

This demand caught the songwriter completely by surprise. Newbury had never sung "Dixie" during a show and had no plans to add it to his act. Yet for a young man who was proud of his southern roots, the warning also got under his skin. As he prepared to go onstage, he found himself wondering, "What's wrong with singing 'Dixie'?"

"I felt that 'Dixie' was *not* a racist song," Newbury explained. "It had been written by a man from New York. I didn't feel it was right that people had taken this old folk song and changed its meaning so that it was now considered inflammatory. So, in an attempt to change those views, I decided to sing the song, but in a different way, as a ballad."

As he walked onstage the songwriter knew he was going to put "Dixie" into his set. He also realized that this decision flew in the face of good logic and might cost him future bookings at the well-known club. Those who frequented the Bitter End were usually young and liberal, more likely to burn draft cards than cheer a country song. So not only would the club's manager be upset at Newbury's defying his orders, but the audience might also greet "Dixie" with catcalls or worse. Yet

31

even if that was the case, the songwriter felt as if the Lord himself was nudging him to sing "Dixie," and Mickey was not going to refuse the Lord's request.

Newbury was about halfway through his show when he decided to insert the old folk song in his set. With just his guitar for accompaniment, the Texan mournfully wrapped his voice around each phrase of the old song.

> I wish I was in the land of cotton,
> Old times there are not forgotten,
> Look away, look away, look away, Dixieland.
>
> Oh I wish I was in Dixie,
>
> Away, Away,
> Away down south in the land of cotton,
> Away down south in Dixie,
>
> In Dixieland where I was born,
>
> Early, Lord, one frosty morn,
> Look away, look away, look away, Dixieland.

As he sang, the Bitter End became so quiet it was almost as if the audience was in a trance. As he finished the only verse he knew to the South's most famous folk tune, Mickey felt a need to expand upon the moment.

"I don't know why," Newbury explained, "but I just moved naturally from 'Dixie' to 'Battle Hymn of the Republic.'"

> Glory! glory, hallelujah! Glory! glory, hallelujah!
> Glory! glory, hallelujah! His truth is marching on.

Julia Ward Howe, who had penned "Battle Hymn of the Republic" during the first days of the Civil War, probably would have loved Newbury's simple and direct approach. When Mickey sang the gospel hymn, it was not a march but a prayer. Politicians and preachers had tried for years to accomplish what the singer was now so easily doing by combining two familiar songs. For the moment, as the song of the North meshed with the song of the South, there was a peace in the room that belied the problems that were then dividing the nation. Within moments, all those at the Bitter End seemed to feel a kinship to those around them.

Newbury's God-given inspiration did not stop when he'd torn down the musical Mason-Dixon line by uniting "Dixie" and "Battle Hymn of the Republic." As he finished the latter with, "His truth is marching on," the songwriter immediately began singing a Negro slave spiritual.

> So hush little baby, don't you cry,
> You know your daddy's bound to die,
> But all my trials, Lord, will soon be over.

"All My Trials" completed the story begun with "Dixie." Three songs that so defined the groups who fought and suffered through the Civil War and its legacy had now been brought together in one place by one man. It was a moment of great inspiration and healing as songs that had once caused strong emotions that divided people now brought them to a place where they could reach out to each other. As he left the stage that night, the songwriter began to believe that the words in Martin Luther King's 1963 "I Have a Dream" speech might well come true in his lifetime.

As would have seemed natural, Newbury recorded his "American Trilogy." Yet except for the first night at the Bitter

End, the song did not seem to work with audiences. Radio stations that played it received complaints from both liberals and conservatives. Many blacks resented having a traditional Negro spiritual linked with "Dixie," and many whites didn't want "Dixie" tied to either "All My Trials" or "Battle Hymn of the Republic." Additionally, a host of Christian groups did not like the fact that a gospel song had been used as a bridge between two folk songs. With the press hounding him during every interview, Newbury gave up on the song he thought had been given to him by God. A second chance for "An American Trilogy" would come at a moment when few were awake to hear it.

In the early 1970s, when television stations still signed off by playing "The National Anthem," a Memphis station decided to end its day's broadcast with Newbury's "An American Trilogy." The song was coupled to images of patriotic American scenes. Priscilla Presley was watching that evening and became so caught up in Newbury's performance that she called the station to get a copy of the recording. Priscilla shared that copy with her husband, Elvis, and within a few weeks rock and roll's king was singing "An American Trilogy" onstage.

"When Elvis sang it and recorded it," Newbury explained, "it saved the song. When he sang it, people understood the message. He was probably the only one in the world who could have made it work."

Thanks to Elvis, Newbury's inspirational arrangement began to inspire other vocalists from every facet of entertainment to cut "An American Trilogy." Almost a hundred artists including Led Zeppelin, Enrique Chia, the Osmonds,

Randy Travis, Tanzorchester Klaus Hallen, and even the London Symphony Orchestra have recorded it. It has been performed around the world and has become the song many believe defines the total American experience better than any other. To millions "An American Trilogy" shows what can happen when faith and forgiveness are allowed to expose and heal past wounds.

"Faith," Newbury explained, "is something we cannot see, but it is real. Have faith, for nothing on this earth but your fear can harm you."

"An American Trilogy" is now one of the nation's most powerful and joyful songs of faith. It is a song that has built a bridge that connects all elements of the American experience. It is also a song that shows what can happen when God is allowed to work directly in one man's life. Mickey Newbury accepted the Lord's charge and had the courage to present that inspiration in front of a crowd seemingly not ready to accept a message of reconciliation and healing. Newbury not only touched that crowd by following his God-given call, but he has touched millions each year since that night. "An American Trilogy" stands as a monument to faith put into action, and it provides a clear picture of how forgiveness can initiate healing.

BATTLE HYMN OF THE REPUBLIC

She is best remembered as the writer of "Battle Hymn of the Republic," and fittingly so, because Julia Ward Howe was a fighter, a woman who would put her life and reputation on the line to support causes in which she deeply believed. So while her "Battle Hymn" was written for a specific time and a specific cause, the verses that inspired a nation during the Civil War could easily define this woman's entire life. Until the day she died, Howe lived the words, "His truth is marching on," and more than nine decades later those words still ring true in American hearts.

To say this woman did not have a profound effect on the history of the United States would be like saying Babe Ruth was a pretty fair hitter. Howe once told a convention audience, "The strokes of the pen need deliberation as much as the sword needs swiftness." Whenever she spoke or wrote, Howe chose what she said very carefully. While she was a woman of action, she also realized that the words she wrote or said could have an impact far beyond any single step or action she took. So it was because of her words that the woman had such great influence.

That influence was a driving force behind the abolition of slavery, the right of women to vote, government programs to care for the poor and underrepresented, prison reform, and even the holiday that honors mothers. Though small in stature, to those she touched and the world she so dramatically shaped with her ideas and words, Howe was a giant. Yet it was while riding in a carriage during the Civil War that Howe accepted a challenge that brought forth one of the greatest songs of all time—and perhaps her most meaningful gift to the world.

Julia Ward was born into a wealthy New York City family and, because of the fortune of being born into such a family, she was given the rare opportunity to gain an education equal to that of the boys of her day. In 1841 Julia was traveling to Boston on a family outing. On the trip she met noted philanthropist and educator, Samuel G. Howe—founder of the Perkins Institute for the Blind, and the first man to teach a blind and deaf woman to speak. Though separated by more than two decades in age, Julia and Samuel were kindred spirits. They married on April 23, 1843, and settled in Boston. From the beginning of this union, the very progressive-thinking Howe fully and enthusiastically supported his wife's desire to pursue a writing career. He felt the world needed to hear her thoughts, ideas, and vision for America. Samuel was quickly proven right as within a year Julia gained a national following penning courageous commentaries for the antislavery periodical, the *Commonwealth*.

For more than a decade Julia, who rose to the rank of publisher of the *Commonwealth*, composed editorials, poetry, stories, and witty features for scores of publications. She also published books such as *Passion Flowers*, *Words of the Hours*, and *A Trip to Cuba*. Her acclaim as a public speaker created a constant demand for speaking engagements. Her many treks increased when the Civil War broke out. Traveling throughout New England, Howe gave scores of lectures and directed aid drives for the cause

Mine eyes have seen the glory of the coming of the Lord;
He is trampling out the vintage where the grapes of wrath are
  stored;
He hath loosed the fateful lightning of His terrible swift sword;
His truth is marching on.

Chorus:
Glory! glory, hallelujah! Glory! glory, hallelujah!
Glory! glory, hallelujah! His truth is marching on.

I have seen Him in the watchfires of a hundred circling camps;
They have builded Him an altar in the evening dews and damps;
I can read His righteous sentence by the dim and flaring lamps;
His day is marching on.

Chorus

I have read a fiery gospel; writ in burnished rows of steel
"As you deal with my contemners, so with you my grace shall
  deal,"
Let the Hero born of woman crush the serpent with His heel:
Since God is marching on!

Chorus

He has sounded forth the trumpet that shall never sound retreat;
He is sifting out the hearts of men before His judgment seat;
O be swift, my soul, to answer Him! be jubilant, my feet!
Our God is marching on.

Chorus

In the beauty of the lilies Christ was born across the sea,
With a glory in His bosom that transfigures you and me;
As He died to make men holy, let us die to make men free;
While God is marching on.

Chorus

of the federal government. This work led her to Washington in 1861, and her passion for serving her nation was the reason she was in the right place at the right time to compose one of America's most loved hymns.

It was a warm night when Julia Ward Howe rode through the nation's capital with her husband; a minister friend, Dr. James Freeman Clarke; and Governor Andrews of Massachusetts. Dr. Howe had been placed in charge of the military's medical department. He had already seen firsthand the bloodbath of close fighting. He knew too well the smell of death and the screams of those badly injured. The doctor told his carriage companions that the worst was still ahead. This would be a long and bloody war. The others in the coach were now realizing these facts for the first time.

As the group rode along the narrow streets, Julia noted the tents and campfires that seemed to occupy every small patch of ground in and around Washington. Blue-clad troops appeared to be everywhere. Many looked scared, more than a few were drunk, and all of them seemed intent on making the most of the days before they were sent off to fight the soldiers in gray. With men shouting, cursing, and shooting guns in the air, the lone woman in the coach wondered if the whole world had gone mad.

As the party slowly made its way along Washington's crowded streets, they heard a group of men singing the song "John Brown's Body." Rather than inspiring patriotic spirit in the visitors, the lyrics that talked about a man rotting in the soil brought disgust. Dr. Clarke even looked over at Mrs. Howe and said, "Surely there are better words for such a wonderful tune." Though none of the men thought any more about the observation, the woman in the carriage was now haunted by the melody and its terribly macabre lyrics.

It was a depressed Julia Howe who climbed into her hotel bed that night. Although she was exhausted, she was unable to think of anything but the pain and suffering her husband assured her would soon be visiting every household in the former United States. In the dark and unfamiliar room, those images of war somehow merged with the tune to "John Brown's Body." When this happened, inspiration took hold.

"This soul-inspiring song was the incarnation of patriotic and martial feeling," she later told an audience. "It was struck out of the white heat of unconscious inspiration, the soul's product of a mighty movement. It is the most resonant and elevating of all America's battle hymns."

Getting out of bed, Howe picked up a pencil and paper and began to jot down her thoughts. Within seconds she had written a new first verse to the old tune.

Mine eyes have seen the glory of the coming of the Lord;
He is trampling out the vintage where the grapes of wrath are stored;
He hath loosed the fateful lightning of His terrible swift sword;
His truth is marching on.

At daybreak, Howe woke her husband and sang the finished song to him. Deeply moved, Dr. Howe agreed that his wife had been truly inspired. The couple felt that with a little work this could be a song that would spur the Union toward victory. Over the next few days, Julia worked out the rough spots and added another verse. A week later, when she returned to her home in Boston, Julia sent "Mine

Eyes Have Seen the Glory" to the *Atlantic Monthly*. In early 1862 the magazine brought Julia's song to America's public.

The response was so great that "Battle Hymn" or "Marching On" was quickly reprinted in numerous magazines and newspapers. President Lincoln was so moved by the new song that he wrote Howe a letter and declared to the press that, in spite of the fact that the tune had been composed in the South before the war, this was his new favorite song. Lincoln even asked that the marine band play it every time they were in his presence. Not surprisingly, considering how quickly the song had been adopted by politicians and civilians, Union troops marched to "Battle Hymn of the Republic" for the remainder of the war. It was also heard several times the day Lee surrendered to Grant, and it was played during Lincoln's funeral procession.

Julia Ward Howe had written the song to inspire the Union during the Civil War. When that war ended and the Union again included all the states, Howe's song should have disappeared, as did hundreds of other Civil War ballads. Yet largely thanks to the woman and the causes she undertook for the rest of her life, "Battle Hymn of the Republic" lived on.

Howe realized that just freeing Negro slaves did not make these men and women equal in the eyes of most Americans in the North or the South. She knew that without education and financial help, a majority of black Americans would be little better off as free people than they had been when they were property. So in an effort to help gain rights for these newly freed citizens, Howe wrote and spoke about the needs of the American Negro. A devoutly religious woman, she almost always put her thoughts into the context of her faith, as she had with "Battle Hymn."

"I think nothing is religion that puts one individual absolutely above others," she told one audience as she spoke on both minority and women's rights, "and surely nothing is religion that puts one sex above another. Religion is primarily our relation to the Supreme, to God himself. It is for him to judge; it is for him to say where we belong, who is highest and who is not; of that we know nothing. And any religion that will sacrifice a certain set of human beings for the enjoyment or aggrandizement or advantage of another is no religion. It is a thing that may be allowed, but it is against true religion. Any religion that sacrifices women to the brutality of men is no religion."

While the Civil War was over, Howe's march for truth was really just beginning. To help promote her causes, she founded the New England women's club. She also presided over the American Woman-Suffrage Association. In 1872 she traveled to London and spoke at the World's Prison Reform Congress. She went back to England later that year to preside over the founding of the Woman's Peace Association. When not speaking out on important moral causes in the United States and Britain, she filled pulpits in Rome, Italy, and Santo Domingo, and lectured at the Concord School of

Philosophy. Everywhere she went she was greeted by "Battle Hymn of the Republic." Without Howe's direct involvement in these efforts, it is doubtful that the Civil War standard would ever have been recognized as such a powerful voice for all who sought freedom. Yet soon this song was attached to every cause that demanded liberty and human rights.

In her old age Howe continued to fight for freedom and justice. It was a job she considered an honor, a duty she thought of as a blessing, and a task she relished.

"The bowl of life grows sweeter as I drink it," she told a group in 1908. "All the sugar is at the bottom." Life might have tasted so sweet to Howe because so much of what she promoted she watched come to fruition.

The first woman elected to the American Academy of Arts and Letters, the force behind women's suffrage, abolition of slavery, prison reform, and equal rights, died at her home in 1910. While she knew she had changed the world with her words and actions, it probably would have surprised even Howe that her "Battle Hymn" was picked up a generation later by the daughter of a New Orleans stevedore and became the marching song of the Civil Rights movement. Howe would have loved to hear Mahalia Jackson bring that song to a new fight and a new generation. The writer would have been thrilled that a child of the South had rallied millions of others, both black and white, men and women, to gain rights won during the Civil War but not fully realized until more than a century later.

Just before she died in 1910, Julia Ward Howe was asked about her "Battle Hymn of the Republic." She thought for a moment, then, using carefully chosen words, said, "The wild echoes of that fearful struggle have long since died away, and with them all memories of unkindness between ourselves and our Southern brethren. But those who once loved my hymn still sing it. I hope and believe that it stands for what our whole country now believes in—that is, the sacredness of human liberty. My poem did some service in the Civil War. I wish very much that it may do good service in peace, which I pray God, may never be broken."

Though her prayer for a lasting peace was not answered, Howe's song has sustained not only Americans but men and women all over the world during both war and peace. When the great leader of World War II Britain died, his passing was noted in every corner of the globe. Millions watched Winston Churchill's funeral on television or listened to the proceedings on radio. For many the most surprising moment of the service was when a choir sang "Battle Hymn of the Republic." It seemed that Churchill loved the uniquely American hymn because it spelled out so clearly what each Christian should try to do in life—find a just cause and fight to assure victory for that cause.

That is how Churchill wanted to be remembered, and there can be no doubt that this is how Julia Ward Howe should and will always be remembered. Howe did not just write "Battle Hymn of the Republic," she lived it!

ETERNAL FATHER,
STRONG TO SAVE
(THE NAVY HYMN)

The "Marine's Hymn" is by far the best-known United States service song, but it is the U.S. Navy that lays claim to one of the most moving spiritual anthems as its official hymn. While the song has evolved into a prayer for men who guard America's oceans, and while it was inspired by the power of the sea, "Eternal Father, Strong to Save" was not written by an American. It was actually first claimed by England's Royal Navy and not the men and women flying the Stars and Stripes. Yet because of two traumatic events, most Americans have come to think of "Eternal Father, Strong to Save" as one of this country's most hallowed pieces of patriotic music.

William Whiting was born in Kensington, Middlesex, England, on November 1, 1825. A bright child with a natural flair for music, Whiting was educated at Clapham and Winchester Colleges. He graduated with honors and was appointed the director of Winchester music school while still in his twenties. Yet if not for a perilous experience while sailing on the Mediterranean and the fears experienced by one of his students, Whiting probably would now be long forgotten.

The schoolmaster had actually grown up on the coast. As a child he had splashed in the waves, run along beaches, and greeted fishermen as they returned home to port. The smell of salt water, the beauty of the waves, and the poetic sounds of the ocean were a part of his being. Because of the experiences of his childhood, he believed he knew well the power of the ocean. This belief was challenged when, at the age of thirty-five, he found himself in the midst of a storm that seemed determined to send him to the bottom of the sea. It was a day he would never forget.

The storm had come up quickly and had taken on all the violence normally associated with a hurricane. For hours the crew of the ship on which Whiting was sailing fought wind and waves, but no matter what they did the water always seemed to win. The furious storm didn't just demand their attention, it seemed to relish toying with the men, tossing them about like a dog playing with an old rag. Brave sailors were crying, and heathen old salts had fallen to their knees in prayer. Whiting must have felt like John Newton, the writer of "Amazing Grace," who was inspired to write that great hymn after surviving a similar storm. In both cases each man made his peace with God and waited for the end.

Prayer was natural for Whiting. He lived his faith; it was a part of every facet of his life. During the storm he prayed for personal help and guidance, even as he prayed for the men who courageously tried everything in their power to keep the ship afloat. Yet Whiting ultimately knew that in times like these only God had the power to save them. The schoolmaster also was firm in his conviction that he had really been saved when he had accepted Christ as his Savior many years before. Secure in his ultimate salvation, Whiting hung onto a rail and watched the mighty sea pound the man-made craft. While others around him wept and begged, Whiting calmly observed the power that man could not control. Over the next few hours thousands of different images were clearly recorded, pressed into his memory like keepsakes in a scrapbook.

Whiting and the ship survived that day, and their vessel, though damaged, made it back to port. Yet, as he later told his friends, the schoolmaster would never again look at the ocean in the same way. The power of the water he had witnessed in the storm would be evident to him even on the most serene morning tide. From that time on he respected the ocean almost as much as he respected the God who ruled over it.

In 1860 a Winchester student came to Whiting to reveal a secret. The young man had just visited England's second largest port, Southampton. He had watched the ships come and go and had observed hundreds of happy passengers disembark and other eager men and women board these ships. Yet as he looked out to the west and studied the rising and falling waves, clouds of doubt filled his mind. He found himself scared to death of the water, afraid of unseen monsters that might be waiting for him if he should ever have to sail. As long as his fears remained just personal nightmares, the student could deal with them. But now he had a ticket in his hand for America. He could no longer run from the dreams that haunted him at night.

Whiting reassured the young man that he would be fine. He then told him about his experiences on the water, including the one in the storm. The schoolmaster assured the student that God would be with him even as he sailed over the deepest, darkest waves. The older man then stated that no storm could possibly overpower the mighty Lord. Finally, as he sent the boy away, Whiting made him a promise: "Before

Eternal Father, Strong to save,
Whose arm hath bound the restless wave,
Who bid'st the mighty Ocean deep
Its own appointed limits keep;
O hear us when we cry to Thee,
For those in peril on the sea.

O Christ! Whose voice the waters heard
And hushed their raging at Thy word,
Who walked'st on the foaming deep,
And calm amidst its rage didst sleep;
Oh hear us when we cry to Thee
For those in peril on the sea!

Most Holy spirit! Who didst brood
Upon the chaos dark and rude,
And bid its angry tumult cease,
And give, for wild confusion, peace;
Oh, hear us when we cry to Thee
For those in peril on the sea!

O Trinity of love and power!
Our brethren shield in danger's hour;
From rock and tempest, fire and foe,
Protect them wheresoe'er they go;
Thus evermore shall rise to Thee,
Glad hymns of praise from land and sea.

you depart, I will give you something to anchor your faith."

Drawing from his own experiences, Whiting wrote a poem. Combining his deep faith with the power and majesty he observed in the sea, the schoolmaster penned several stanzas of verse he called "Eternal Father, Strong to Save." The teacher gave the frightened student a copy to carry with him on his journey. Though no one realized it then, the words that would become America's most beloved sacred service hymn arrived in the United States in 1860 in the hands of a young man very happy to finally put his feet on solid ground.

Meanwhile John B. Dykes, a vicar who would eventually compose the music to hundreds of hymns, had just finished his doctorate in divinity from Durhman University in England when he was given a copy of Whiting's poem in some correspondence from a friend. When Dykes was told by this friend that Whiting's inspiration for the song had come from a near fatal voyage on the Mediterranean Sea, the vicar began to leaf through his personal music files. Buried behind Dyke's compositions "Holy, Holy, Holy" and "Jesus Lover of My Soul" was a tune called "Melita." Melita was the ancient name for the Mediterranean Island of Malta. Playing the music through on his organ, Dykes discovered that Whiting's "Eternal Father,

Strong to Save" fit the melody note for note and
line for line. It was as if the poem and music had been written
for each other. The song was published later that year.

"Eternal Father" was quickly picked up by the English
Navy. Many captains ordered the hymn to be sung during the morning; others had it sung at the close of the
day. As British sailors carried the song around the globe,
other nations discovered it. In 1879 Lieutenant Commander Charles Jackson of the United States Navy heard
the English hymn in England. Jackson brought "Eternal
Father" back to the Naval Academy, where it was initially
sung in chapel by the Midshipman Choir. Later in the
same year the Academy began the practice of conclud-
ing each Sunday's church services by singing the first
verse of this hymn. In a sense, "Eternal Father, Strong to
Save" became a Christian "Taps" for those wearing U.S.
Navy blue.

By the beginning of the twentieth century, United States
sailors were singing the first verse of "Eternal Father" on
every ship in the navy. In most cases the service branch's
hymn was played each day when ships were at sea. Its
words were memorized by officers and enlisted men. While
"Anchors Away" was often performed with humor, "Eternal Father, Strong to Save" was treated with all the respect
usually reserved for "The Star-Spangled Banner."

By the end of World War I, "Eternal Father" had become
known as "The Navy Hymn." During World War II, the
hymn was not only used as a part of daily routine but
became the song most used during burials at sea. If there
was not a band present to play the anthem or a record

available of "The Navy Hymn," it was sung a cappella by the crew or the commanding officer simply read Whiting's words. No final farewell was complete without the poem being used in some way.

When meeting with England's Winston Churchill at the beginning of the American involvement in the Second World War, President Franklin D. Roosevelt asked for "Eternal Father" to be played at the close of the leaders' final face-to-face session. Four years later, when FDR died, "The Navy Hymn" was sung at the president's funeral at Hyde Park, New York. The song written by an Englishman would become even better known in the United States when it was performed as the body of President John F. Kennedy was carried up the steps of the Capitol to lie in state in November of 1963. "Eternal Father" was also played when JFK's body was lowered into its grave.

The founding fathers were so adamant about the separation of church and state that many argued there should be no chaplains allowed into the chambers of the House or Senate and that faith and government maintain friendly but distant ties. Even the use of "In God We Trust" was not allowed on American currency until 1864. Yet the popularity of "Eternal Father, Strong to Save" proves that God can go wherever he chooses, and in times of tribulation people will reach out to him. Written for a young man who was scared of the water, the only William Whiting poem to become a song still comforts those who need to know that a power greater than all the forces on earth can not only reach out to them but save them in the air, on land, and at sea.

FAITH OF OUR FATHERS

*I*n April 1945 the United States of America had a great deal for which to be thankful. The war in Europe was winding down, and the Japanese were retreating in the Pacific. There seemed to be little doubt that the Axis powers would be defeated by the end of the year. The only real question haunting everyone from the president to military leaders to servicemen to the families and friends waiting at home was how many more Americans would die before peace was finally achieved. But in general, optimism was everywhere as the mood in the United States was the most upbeat it had been in years.

A little more than a week later, however, another tragedy struck the nation and caused a confident America to be badly shaken. Franklin D. Roosevelt died suddenly. For a country that had no idea their president had been sick, this was indeed shocking news, and it sent Americans into a state of mourning.

Any time a president dies in office, people's faith in their government is tested. Yet what compounded this dilemma in the waning days of World War II was just how much America had come to depend upon FDR. He was not just another president; the New Yorker had been in office for three full terms and had just begun his fourth. He had led the nation through the Great Depression with his faith, grit, determination, and innovative social programs. It was only natural that millions believed it was the president who had willed the United States through the most turbulent economic period in its history.

Then, when the Japanese had bombed Pearl Harbor, sending the country headlong into another world war, FDR had been the man in charge of this fight as well. While the United States was thunderstruck when the news of Roosevelt's death echoed across the land, the rest of the free world was perhaps even more deeply shaken. FDR had literally become the leader of the free world. He was viewed almost as a superman by some Europeans. Many even questioned if the tide of war would turn in favor of the Axis without FDR in charge of America. For those who had been in the midst of the European fighting for years, it was a time of terrible insecurity. Never before had an American president meant so much to so many beyond the shores of the United States.

Roosevelt had been the first United States politician to use the power of radio. He had spoken directly to the American people through this new medium since coming into office in 1933. Time and time again his strong, calm voice had reassured citizens, almost like a father would reassure a child, that things were going to be all right. Now it was radio that brought the president's memorial and funeral into the homes of those who had grown so dependent upon his guidance. As millions stopped what they were doing to say a final farewell on April 14, 1945, a song the president himself had picked for the service lifted the spirits of millions. This song reminded America that its fight for freedom would continue. While this old hymn was used that day to bolster the faith of the people of the United States, the song was actually written to memorialize a far different moment in history and vastly different men who became heroes of faith.

Faith of our fathers! living still
In spite of dungeon, fire and sword:
O how our hearts beat high with joy
Whene'er we hear that glorious word!
Faith of our fathers, holy faith!
We will be true to thee till death!

Our fathers, chained in prisons dark,
Were still in heart and conscience free:
How sweet would be their children's fate,
If they, like them, could die for thee!
Faith of our fathers, holy faith!
We will be true to thee till death!

Faith of our fathers! we will love
Both friend and foe in all our strife:
And preach thee, too, as love knows how,
By kindly words and virtuous life:
Faith of our fathers, holy
faith!
We will be true to thee
till death!

At one time Frederick W. Faber was one of the most ardent clerics in the Church of England. The dynamic man from Calverly, England, began his ministry after graduating from Oxford in 1843. Yet even as he quickly rose up the ranks in the Anglican Church, he began to question Britain's treatment of Catholics. As the firm hand of the nation's official church cracked down harder on those who practiced Catholicism, Faber stood up for the rights of individuals to freely choose their faith. He pointed to other countries, including the United States, where religion thrived because the state did not favor one faith over another. Finally, when he determined that he could not influence the Anglican Church or British government to change its rigid rules, he did the unthinkable—he gave up his position in the Church of England and became a Catholic priest.

As a Catholic, Faber continued his fight for the right to worship freely. He not only preached this message from his pulpit but also lobbied the government for that right. Yet more than his sermons and his petitions, it was in music that Faber's voice made the deepest impression. One of his more than one hundred hymns, "Faith of Our Fathers" was written to remind Catholics of all those who had died for their faith during persecution under King Henry VIII. Published in 1849, "Faith of Our Fathers" quickly became one of the best-loved Catholic hymns in both England and Ireland, opening the door for a new kind of song being used in worship services. Within a decade, Faber's song had made it to the United States, where it was adopted not only by Catholics but by almost all other Christian denominations.

By the twentieth century the original meaning of "Faith of Our Fathers" had been all but forgotten by most who sang the hymn. In the United States, where the hymn was usually used in church services to commemorate Independence Day, the song was almost always connected with the early American settlers, the faith of the pilgrims, and the examples of the men who fought and died for freedom during the Revolutionary War. That is the way the song continued to be thought of until that spring day in 1845 when millions listened to it during FDR's funeral.

For the generation of Americans who survived the Great Depression and were then winning the war against Germany and Japan, the inclusion of "Faith of Our Fathers" seemed the perfect choice for that very dark moment in time. Americans had been stunned by the passing of the world's most powerful leader, yet the song Roosevelt had chosen for his own funeral seemed to state very clearly that while the man had died, faith lived on.

Because of its use at FDR's funeral, "Faith of Our Fathers" became an even more beloved and used hymn in America. For millions Frederick Faber's lyrics still serve as a reminder that faith does not die even when men give their lives to preserve it. Millions of Americans have died to insure that freedom of worship—the ability to freely express faith—is not only a promise in the U.S. but also a guarantee. Though written for an entirely different reason, perhaps no song better reminds Americans of this fact than "Faith of Our Fathers."

GOD BLESS AMERICA

*I*rving Berlin has been called "America's greatest song-writer." In his century of living he composed thousands of songs and hundreds of hits including "White Christmas," "Fools Fall in Love," "Puttin' on the Ritz," and "This Is the Army, Mr. Jones." Just based on the sheer volume of his recorded work, there can be little doubt that the small immigrant from Russia penned more classics than any other popular songwriter. Yet of all the incredible compositions that carry his name, late in life the composer said one song stood out head and shoulders above the rest. The work Berlin considered his greatest was "God Bless America." While it seems clear that no patriotic hymn is as universally loved by Americans as this song, it is ironic that Berlin came to think of it so highly, because "God Bless America" would never have made it out of the composer's rejected song pile if it had not been for an enthusiastic radio personality.

By the time she was nine years old, little Kate Smith already had the voice of a full-grown woman. When she opened her mouth to sing, the sounds that came forth were not just beautiful, they were sung with a spirit and force that indicated music was more than just a hobby for this child, it was obviously her passion. Kate so loved to sing that her mother constantly looked for places to show off her little girl. When Mrs. Smith found a way to get Kate on a stage in or around her hometown of Washington D.C., the girl's huge smile, bright eyes, and incredible talent stole the spotlight from every other act on the bill. She loved to sing so much that she performed anywhere someone would give her a place on a program, including Catholic church fundraisers, community fairs, talent shows, and the war bond rallies of World War I.

One night, while Smith belted out a stirring rendition of the new hit song "Over There," an awed General John J. "Blackjack" Pershing sat spellbound in the audience. Before she ever got to the first chorus, the army's commanding officer had become Smith's biggest fan. Within a week of that performance, Pershing took Kate to the White House, where she sang for President Warren G. Harding. Harding gave Smith a small medal for her bond-raising efforts and encouraged her to continue to use her vocal talents. The little girl figured she *had* to do what the most powerful man in the United States instructed, so she never quit singing.

In 1926 a nineteen-year-old Smith landed a spot on the bill at the Earle Theater. She was no longer a cute little kid. Her body size now matched her huge voice. While the vaudeville crowds enjoyed her music, comics almost always followed her performance with cruel jokes and pointed jabs aimed at her well-rounded form. This night-after-night humiliation grew so great that the singer almost quit performing and returned to college. Yet when the devoutly religious Smith prayed her daily prayers, she felt the hand of God pushing her back onto the stage. It was as if he were trying to assure her that singing was her calling in life. Because of this, she felt that if she ever gave up on her musical career, she would never have the opportunity to achieve what the Lord had placed her on the earth to accomplish. Though the jokes and jabs continued to be tossed her way in machine-gun-like fashion, Kate now chose to laugh with her detractors rather than run away and cry by herself. Her courage in the face of ridicule paid off in 1929. Thanks to her proven talent and her obviously positive attitude, Smith landed a role on Broadway and signed a recording contract with Columbia Records. At 260 pounds she was now truly the biggest female act in the Big Apple.

Though she gained a great following onstage, it would be the new medium of radio that made Smith a national star. In 1931, the same year her self-penned "When the Moon Comes Over the Mountain" became a huge hit, CBS gave Kate her own weekly show. As the network soon discovered, Smith's sincere personality, enthusiastic spirit, robust voice, and quick wit were perfectly suited for radio. She instantly became one of the medium's brightest acts. Kate was so personable that people quickly adopted her as if she were a member of their own family. Her fans, who numbered in the millions, wrote her letters, sent her wires, and even prayed for her. It seemed that, like a ray of sunshine, Smith simply made people feel good.

Perhaps no entertainer of any era has ever felt a greater responsibility to her fans than did Kate Smith. She realized that her loyal audience, the ones who listened to her radio programs and bought her records, had made her a very rich woman while also allowing her to do what she believed she was called to do. She felt so humbled by this that she spent much of her life trying to find ways to give special gifts back to those who had made her American Dream come true.

This need to give back to her public led her to become one of the first radio entertainers to reach out to soldiers and veterans. It was probably no accident that Kate's desire to say thank you to these men who served their country led to her introducing America to one of its most beloved songs.

Smith wanted to do something special for her Armistice Day (now Veteran's Day) program. She felt a need to sing a patriotic anthem that would reach the hearts of those who had served during World War I. She, her orchestra leaders, members of her band, and her manager began to search for such a song months before the program's scheduled November airdate. They found absolutely nothing. It seemed no one was even attempting to compose songs about loving America during the Great Depression. Yet rather than give up and sing a well-known standard such as "My Country, 'Tis of Thee" or "America, the Beautiful," the ever-determined Smith kept looking. She also started praying. Ultimately it was probably her prayers that paid off.

Irving Berlin visited Europe during the summer of 1937. During his time there the tunesmith could clearly see that the world was headed for another war. He returned to the U.S. hoping to write a song that would somehow motivate Americans to stay out of the next conflict. He did not want to see any more men from his adopted country dying on overseas battlefields. Yet try as he might, he could not find a way to compose anything of market value using the theme of peace. Berlin was still working on the concept when Ted Collins, Smith's manager, stopped by the composer's office in October.

Collins shared with the master songwriter Kate's desire to sing a new patriotic song for her Armistice Day salute. At first Berlin told the manager that he could be of no help. Except for his Broadway musical *Yip! Yip! Yaphank*, a fundraising production that had introduced "This Is the Army, Mr. Jones" during World War I, Berlin had pretty much left patriotic composing to his rival, George M. Cohan. Yet as the men continued to visit, the songwriter recalled a number he had cut out of *Yip! Yip! Yaphank*. Berlin had written the tune as a show closer but had dumped it because he thought it was too sappy for Broadway's sophisticated audiences. As he considered the kind of folks who listened to Kate Smith, he began to believe the old throwaway song might now work. Collins and Berlin swapped entertainment stories as the songwriter's secretary searched through hundreds of rejected scores trying to find something Berlin called "God Bless America." Hours later, by the time she finally discovered the music in the bottom of an old trunk, Collins had gone home.

Berlin studied the faded old manuscript. Upon review he decided it was better than he remembered it being. After playing through it on his office piano, he decided it might just work. Picking up his pencil he rewrote a few lines, then dropped the old march tune in an envelope to be sent to Smith.

As soon as she read "God Bless America," the nation's favorite singer said a quick prayer of thanks. *Yes, this is what I want*, she probably thought as she went back over the opening. *Yes, the storm clouds are gathering across the sea, but with God's help, we can either avoid this conflict or find a way to survive it.* After rehearsing the song with her orchestra a few times, Smith knew this was the perfect song given to her at the perfect time. While she gladly told everyone that Irving Berlin had penned it, the singer really felt this was a musical gift that had come directly from God. It was the answer to the divine call she had felt a decade before, the reason she had never given up in the face of ridicule.

Smith's prime-time program was called *The Kate Smith Hour.* Yet she was so popular that CBS had also given her a spot on their afternoon schedule each day. Though she did not debut "God Bless America" until that evening, on the afternoon of Armistice Day she talked about the song on *Kate Smith Speaks.*

"When I first tried [to sing] it over," Smith told the millions who had tuned in that day, "I felt, here is a song that will be timeless—it will never die—others will thrill to its beauty long after we are gone. In my humble estimation, this is the greatest song Irving Berlin has ever composed. It shall be my happy privilege to introduce that song on my program this evening, dedicating it to our American heroes of the World War. As I stand before the microphone and sing it with all my heart, I'll be thinking of our veterans, and I'll be praying with every breath I draw that we shall never have another war."

At 12:13 A.M., eastern time, the Songbird of the South strolled to her CBS microphone, took a deep breath, and said, "And now it is my very great privilege to sing you a song that's never been sung before by anybody and that was written especially for me by one of the greatest composers in the music field today. It's something more than a song—I feel it's one of the most beautiful compositions ever written, a song that will never die. The author, Mr. Irving Berlin. The title, 'God Bless America.'"

Smith probably did think the song had been written for her. Neither her manager nor Berlin had explained that it had been yanked from an old Broadway musical. Yet even if she somehow knew that "God Bless America" had been composed and dismissed in 1917, she still would have honestly felt that God had always intended for her to give this musical gift to the people of the United States. In Smith's mind it was her destiny. And on the air that first evening, she sang the song like the answered prayer she knew it was.

Nick Kenny wrote in the *New York Sunday Mirror*, "I wonder if I ever received as big a thrill as I did last Thursday listening to Kate Smith's inspiring singing of Irving Berlin's new patriotic hymn." Millions of Americans agreed, calling CBS and demanding an encore. Even FDR commented on it. Within twenty-four hours "God Bless America" had become one of the best-known and most-loved songs in the nation. All this in spite of the fact that it had aired but a single time and there was no recording of the song anywhere.

Though her record label would have loved to have had Smith immediately cut a single of Berlin's "new" song, she was not completely satisfied with it. She was in reality a ballad singer, and "God Bless America" had been written as a march tune. So Smith reworked the arrangement into a flowing American balladlike tribute that was pure Kate. She sang this version on radio for the first time on November 24, 1938. It was this arrangement that she performed the rest of her life.

Over the course of the next decade Smith sang "God Bless America" thousands of times. She never grew tired of it. While scores of artists, including Bing Crosby and Gene Autry, recorded it, the song always belonged to the big woman with the bigger voice. In her mind, and in the hearts of millions of her fans, the Lord had given "God Bless America" to the Songbird of the South and no one else. At the end of World War II in 1945, most of the patriotic standards of the era disappeared, yet Smith's "God Bless America" did not. Even as musical tastes changed, the song remained popular, kept Kate Smith in the public eye, and more important, in the collective American heart. She sang the patriotic standard for every president from FDR to Reagan. She lived long enough to thrill the nation by belting it out a final time during the nation's bicentennial celebration. Even after her death, her version of "God Bless America" would continue to inspire millions because of the sincere, dynamic, and prayerful way Kate had always performed the song.

In 2001 a Canadian, Celine Dion, ushered "God Bless America" into the twenty-first century. In the 1990s

Dion had emerged as one of the world's most important pop singers, a woman whose voice captured the hearts of millions of fans both young and old. With record sales in the tens of millions, Dion ranked alongside Whitney Houston and fellow countrywoman Shania Twain as a megastar. Dion recorded the old Berlin number as a tribute to the victims of September 11, 2001. Yet even though this new version sold millions of copies, older Americans could not help but picture Smith as they listened. Most believed it was still her song and probably always would be.

"God Bless America" may not be the nation's official anthem, but it is probably the country's unofficial patriotic hymn. Seven decades after it was written, this ballad of faith and love of country still packs a powerful punch. Yet "God Bless America" is much more than just another patriotic anthem; it is a tribute to the American Dream realized in the lives of two unique people. Where but America could a Russian-born Jewish songwriter and an overweight Catholic entertainer come together to take a forgotten and dismissed song and make it mean so much to so many?

This great standard was created by a man who knew firsthand the promise and potential of what the United States had to offer. Using grit, determination, talent, and hard work, Irving Berlin not only became one of the most famous and successful artists in his field, but, in doing so, blessed millions through his talents and gifts. Berlin overcame prejudice, poverty, and persecution to give his adopted country songs that will live forever—and one song that has inspired millions through some of the nation's most trying times.

Kate Smith was the object of mean jokes and public ridicule. Most who were treated as she was would have given up. Yet this woman of great faith believed so much in her God-given talents and the promise of America that she persevered. Like Berlin, she overcame the long odds that always seemed to be stacked against her and emerged as one of the world's biggest and brightest stars. Because of Smith's courage and convictions, her determination and her attitude, her generosity and compassion, she was in the position to bring Berlin's finest work to the world. It is very likely that no one would have saved "God Bless America" from the throwaway song bin except Smith, and surely no one could have sung it with as much feeling as she did.

"God Bless America" is therefore a testament not just to Irving Berlin and Kate Smith but to what the United States is for so many—the land of opportunity. With its simple words and uncomplicated tune, "God Bless America" has also become more than a patriotic ballad, it is the musical equivalent of the Statue of Liberty.

GOD BLESS THE U.S.A.

On September 1, 1983, a Korean Air jetliner was bound for Japan. To the passengers and crew it seemed just like another routine flight from the United States to Asia. Yet this plane, with the ironic "super spy" flight identification number 007, would somehow deviate from its assigned course and fly into Russian airspace. Normally this intrusion into Soviet airspace would have not caused much of a problem. The plane's captain would have been warned via radio and corrections would have been quickly instituted. The passengers would not have even realized that the navigational error had occurred.

On this evening, however, the situation unfolded very differently. Tension filled a U.S.S.R. air traffic tracking station. A U.S. spy plane had been spotted in the area. Not long after the American plane was discovered, those watching the radar became confused. They mistakenly identified the Korean Airlines flight as the American military jet. When that blip on the radar screen crossed well into Soviet airspace, a Russian military jet was sent out to scare the spy plane away. For some reason that no one on either side of the operation has ever been able to explain, the Korean pilots either did not receive or did not understand the warning from the Russian jet. When they did not respond, the pilot reacted as if this was a wartime situation and fired a missile at what he evidently believed was an American spy plane. Instead, the missile pierced the hull of the Korean passenger jet. Within seconds 269 people, including sixty-three Americans, were dead. In the midst of a period when the cold war seemed to be ending, there were rumors of hostility in the air.

As news of the incident hit radios, televisions, and newspapers, shock echoed up and down streets on both sides of the Pacific. Americans were outraged. They could not believe a government would have the gall to shoot down a passenger plane. This usually did not happen even in times of war. Congressmen and military leaders demanded that the Russian government explain why the events had occurred. When it became public knowledge that an American spy plane had been in the area the night of the crash, many around the world then wondered why a mission of this type would be conducted in an area where passenger jets flew on a regular basis. Fingers were pointed in every direction, and each involved party probably deserved at least a part of the blame. Yet even when the full story began to find its way to the public, nothing could begin to soothe the pain of those who had needlessly lost loved ones. Realizing it had all been a mistake only made the deaths seem even more tragic and senseless.

In the United States it was the numbers of innocent lives lost that spoke the loudest. The faces and names of the dead were not well-known, so there was no one personality or individual on which the public focused. In Japan, however, the tragedy did have an individual face. In the island nation millions mourned the loss of one of the icons of the rock-and-roll era. Kyu Sakamoto had become the first Japanese singer to top the American pop charts when, in 1963, he scored a number one record with the hauntingly beautiful love ballad "Sukiyaki." Ironically, the events that triggered the death of Sakamoto inspired a new song that became more popular in America than even the timeless "Sukiyaki."

Lee Greenwood, the son of a career navy musician and a man who had just recently emerged from years of obscure work as a Vegas act to score a half-dozen country hits, later said that initially the events confused him. Like millions of others he could not believe an accident like this could happen in the advanced technological world of the 1980s. In that sense, when he batted around the fact that so many errors in judgment had been made and so many had died for nothing, the incident took on a proportion that haunted him day and night.

As Greenwood tried to absorb what had happened and the government investigation dug into all the facts to try to pinpoint actual blame, many in America wondered if this was not just another sign of the ineffectiveness and low morale that had seemingly consumed the nation's military machine since Vietnam. It seemed to some that this tragedy pointed to the fact that America had become an impotent force, helpless to protect its friends or even its own. A large part of this feeling could be traced to the Iran hostage situation, when a band of college militants stormed the U.S. embassy in Tehran in November of 1979, holding more than one hundred Americans hostage until January of 1981. As this event was still fresh in people's minds, many tied flight 007 to it. This caused them to become even more depressed and discouraged over the fact that the flag didn't seem to fly as high or mean as much as it once had. To millions both young and old the Korean jet's downing was just one more reminder that the glory days of the nation seemed lost in the past.

As Greenwood sifted through his conflicted thoughts, however, he saw the situation differently. Less than a week after the Russian attack, the singer-songwriter decided the best way to clear his mind and end the confusion was to write out his thoughts on paper. As a musician, he naturally wrote in verse. Yet he hadn't expected the music and words would flow so easily from the jumbled mass of thoughts in his head. Greenwood also was shocked that the song he quickly composed was not about the crash but about his own pride in the nation of his birth. Without meaning to, he had created an American hymn of patriotism and faith.

A decade before the downing of flight 007, the message that poured from the songwriter's mind would not have been embraced. Few were ready to wrap themselves in the flag back then. But now, with patriotic fever and anti-Soviet passions running high, "God Bless the U.S.A." seemed as appropriate as had "God Bless America" during World War II. The powers in Nashville, however, didn't think so. Country record executives and song promoters believed the sentimental standard was simply too sweet and straightforward to have any kind of impact on the charts. Some even thought it would cost Greenwood dearly to release the song as a single. It was predicted that for every person who liked it, several would absolutely hate this syrupy love ballad to the United States.

Jerry Crutchfield, Greenwood's producer, personally liked the song. He even recommended a few changes he felt would make it stronger. Yet even after the rewrite, MCA records passed on recording it. Because Greenwood had just emerged as a major entertainment power, they felt he needed to stick to the formula that had made him a star. They advised him to pitch the song to someone else who had a reputation of flag-waving and stick to the kind of numbers his fans expected.

Greenwood's instincts and drive had kept his faith in his talents alive during his twenty years of climbing the ladder to gain recognition, and he would not listen to those who wanted to sideline his song. As a military brat, he didn't just believe in the song, he believed in everything it said. He felt blessed because of where he was born, he treasured his freedoms, he thanked God for his country, and he was humbled by men like his father who had answered the call to serve America. So rather than bury "God Bless the U.S.A." or give it to another artist, he went to Los Angeles and pitched it personally to the president of MCA Records.

Irving Azoff was shocked to see one of his artists at his front door. He couldn't imagine that any song by a country artist required an impromptu meeting after hours. Nevertheless, he invited Greenwood into his home and listened to the demo record. Azoff liked it, but like all of those in authority in Nashville, he didn't want to cut it now. In a compromise that Greenwood had not been

it would be inappropriate to use the music of the Prussian national anthem in an American celebration. Yet rather than give up on Roberts's lyrics, the group sought outside help. The man who came to their rescue was a self-taught musician from New York City.

George W. Warren, the organist for St. Thomas Church and Columbia University, was commissioned to create a musical movement for Roberts's lyrics that was suited for choral presentation. Considering the grand nature of the patriotic occasion, Warren constructed a musical score that was very different from other hymns of the period. With its unique beginning, a dynamic musical cadence that seemed to pave the way for a vocal explosion, "God of Our Fathers" was an uplifting score that finally matched the message found in its inspired lyrics.

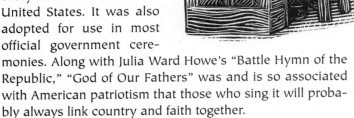

"God of Our Fathers" was introduced at the Constitution centennial celebration as "The National Hymn." The song created an immediate sensation. Because of its reception at its debut, the hymn quickly found its way into the hymnals of almost every denomination in the United States. It was also adopted for use in most official government ceremonies. Along with Julia Ward Howe's "Battle Hymn of the Republic," "God of Our Fathers" was and is so associated with American patriotism that those who sing it will probably always link country and faith together.

When he sat down at his desk in 1876 to look for inspiration for a Fourth of July message, little did Daniel Crane Roberts know that a song meant for one day and one church would come to mean so much to so many for so long. Yet Roberts's contribution to America reflects the true nature of this nation. The most hallowed written gifts given to the United States seem to have always been born in humble circumstances, created not by those seeking fame but by those humbly trying to put into words their feelings about being an American.

HE'S GOT THE WHOLE WORLD IN HIS HANDS

*I*ntroduced to American audiences by Capitol Records, "He's Got the Whole World in His Hands" swept to number one on the country's popular music charts in the spring of 1958. It was a fourteen-year-old boy from England, Laurie London, who brought the black spiritual into America's consciousness.

The arrangement given to London was really a combination of children's hymn and gospel standard, uniting those two separate musical forms into a number that seemed destined more for a Bible school class than success on all the major playlists. Yet this song defied the odds and found a home in the heart of a nation that many felt was turning away from God. During the same period that headlines were screaming, "God Is Dead," "He's Got the Whole World in His Hands" became so popular that it was sung by the likes of Tennessee Ernie Ford and rearranged to meet the needs of some of the top Christian choirs in the world.

The answer to why this song moved from the slave fields of the early South to children's church and then came to mean so much to millions of Americans was probably based more on the insecurity of the era than the actual song itself. For a while in the fifties and early sixties, it seemed that everything was going wrong. People were scared, and even though God was always within reach, most forgot to look for him.

After the close of World War II, when America and its allies had combined forces to conquer the twin threats of Imperial

Japan and Nazi Germany, most Americans felt world security was insured and peace would be long lasting. Yet just a few years after the atom bomb had finally ended the war in the Pacific, another Asian conflict erupted. Suddenly dreams of a world living in harmonious union—fostered by the way the allies of World War II had come together to end the war and promised again by the new United Nations—were shattered. As an iron curtain was being erected in Europe, as Americans began to fight and die in Korea, as Russia built nuclear weapons capable of killing the entire population of the free world, and as the cold war threatened to bring about another much more terrifying world war, the myth of a lasting peace was completely dissolved. An arms race broke out, and newspapers began to run stories on how the two superpowers could literally destroy the world ten times over and still have weapons left for another strike. This news created a subtle change in the way most Americans lived.

Though the era is now often remembered as a carefree time filled with easygoing people and ideal lives, in truth the late fifties and early sixties were a time of great insecurity in the United States. At school students learned to "duck and cover." This was the term used during civil defense drills aimed at trying to ready children for an atomic attack from the U.S.S.R. Families spent thousands of dollars building and stocking bomb shelters in their homes. On television series such as *The Twilight Zone*, Americans were shown what a post-nuclear-war world would look like. In movies Hollywood not only presented World War III in bloody, imaginative films but also invented scores of monsters that supposedly would

He's got the whole world in His hands,
He's got the whole world in His hands,
He's got the whole world in His hands,
He's got the whole world in His hands.

He's got the wind and the rain in His hands,
He's got the wind and the rain in His hands,
He's got the wind and the rain in His hands,
He's got the whole world in His hands.

He's got the tiny little baby in His hands,
He's got the tiny little baby in His hands,
He's got the tiny little baby in His hands,
He's got the whole world in His hands.

He's got you and me, brother, in His hands,
He's got you and me, sister, in His hands,
He's got you and me, brother, in His hands,
He's got the whole world in His hands.

He's got ev'rybody here in His hands,
He's got ev'rybody here in His hands,
He's got ev'rybody here in His hands,
He's got the whole world in His hands.

be the by-product of the atomic age. It seemed to millions of people that if the coming war did not kill them, then giant insects would.

Many Christians believed World War III was just a part of God's plan to destroy the earth by fire. The New Testament book of Revelation became the main source for thousands of sermons and hundreds of books. Preachers of every denomination spoke of mass destruction as if it were coming the very next day, and many believed it was. In scores of places Christian sects retreated to camps to wait for an end of the world they felt would be coming in weeks or months.

This great world instability provided the perfect climate for "He's Got the Whole World in His Hands." People who were looking for any kind of security to latch onto found the very simple message in the song's childlike lyrics a spiritual anchor. The single quickly emerged from obscurity to become a life preserver in the stormy climate of an unsure world. It seemed that simply hearing a child sing the lyrics was a gentle reminder that God was still in control.

In a strange way, "He's Got the Whole in His Hands" was the cold war's equivalent to the Civil War's "Battle Hymn of the Republic." It was a hymn that sustained faith in an environment of doubt. It is therefore not surprising that the song resurfaced on radio stations during the Cuban missile crisis and in the weeks after the assassination of John F. Kennedy. This children's hymn essentially became the "Jesus Loves Me" for a decade's baby boomers.

While "He's Got the Whole World in His Hands" did much to remind people that this was still God's world and he still exercised loving control over people and events, it also helped usher in a new type of Christian music. The simple song inspired a host of other tunes aimed at young people. This new type of hymns, now called praise and worship songs, set into motion a youth revival in the United States. For the first time in history a majority of the new church songs seemed to be aimed at reaching young people with a message of hope and faith. Ultimately this movement grew beyond the church setting and created a new genre called contemporary Christian music.

"He's Got the Whole World in His Hands" first topped the charts because America needed a musical message that God was still in control. It is not surprising, then, that after September 11, 2001, when terror struck American soil for the first time since December 7, 1941, and collective insecurity again rocked the nation as it had in the fifties and early sixties, "He's Got the Whole World in His Hands" came back into the mainstream. In the year following attacks on New York and Washington, D.C., by Al Qaeda, an international terrorist network headed by Osama bin Laden, the song has been recorded scores of times, incorporated into church musicals, arranged into choral anthems, and taught to a new generation of children. The original message remains strong and continues to inspire a nation by touching one person at a time with the reminder that God does have each of us in his hands. In a nation that had built its system of government on the promise that each person is a vital part of the whole, this Christian message is one that continues to have a very special meaning and impact.

How Great Thou Art

hat Carl Boberg knew of the United States he had learned in books and heard in stories. The Swedish preacher never left his native homeland, so his visions of America centered more on cowboys and Indians than they did on music and churches. Yet an unexpected thunderstorm set into motion a series of events that would forever identify the Scandinavian minister's most famous message with the Christian revivals of Dr. Billy Graham and the unique personal faith practiced by Christians in the United States.

"How Great Thou Art" was born in 1880 when a raging rainstorm took Carl Boberg by surprise as he walked through the woods near his home. One minute it had been a beautiful day and the next the skies had opened up and thrust the landscape into chaos. As huge drops of water were pushed by winds that probably exceeded fifty miles per hour, the preacher began to race along a familiar rural path. Soon vicious lightning and awe-inspiring thunder joined the chorus of rain pellets, and a panting Boberg was forced to look for shelter. Spotting a barn, the man rushed inside and shook the water from his hair. From his shelter he watched at the open door as the mighty storm literally took control of everything around him.

For the next fifteen minutes Boberg watched in wonder as the rain continued to pound the earth and dark black clouds swelled across the skies. With a wide-eyed fascination, he absorbed the scene the way a child examines presents under a Christmas tree. Although he had been in rainstorms many times before, it was as if he was observing a storm for the first time in his life. Every detail became important as Boberg noted and felt each change in the wind or rain. What he saw that day was so vivid he managed to record every facet of the experience in his mind.

As quickly as the storm had struck, it dissipated. Except for broken limbs and water clinging to leaves and creating puddles along the road, within ten minutes of the storm's passing almost all signs of destruction and power were gone. They had been replaced by birds singing, a summer sun brightly shining through trees, and a beautiful rainbow shimmering just above the horizon. Stepping back out into this now peaceful world, Boberg slowly began the walk home. Just as he had taken a full accounting of each moment of the storm's brief life, the preacher now examined the wet world around him as if it were all brand new.

Upon arriving home, Boberg sat down at his desk and began to write the story of the storm. For reasons he was never able to understand, his words seemed to naturally come together in verse form. Within an hour he composed nine stanzas of a poem he called "O Store Gud." Before the next Sunday service the pastor matched his lyrics to the meter of an old Swedish folk song. He concluded his message that Sabbath with his inspiring, musical observations of the power of God he had witnessed in a storm and the beauty of God he had seen in the calm scenes that followed. The minister had prayed that "O Store Gud" would strike a spiritual chord with his flock. What he couldn't have guessed was that the song would garner a more positive response than any sermon he had ever given. His congregation even asked him to teach the song to them, and soon it became the small church's most requested hymn.

In the late 1880s, Boberg's "O Store Gud" had been shared with other small congregations and was even published in a Swedish hymnal. It went on to find a place in a few small German songbooks in the early 1900s. By the end of World War II, Boberg's musical message had migrated to Russia. It was there in 1927 that Stuart K. Hine, an English missionary, discovered it. He used the hymn in his services for the next fifteen years, but he never shared the remarkable song with anyone back in Britain. To Hine it was simply a missionary tool to reach non-Christians, not a hymn that had potential for regular English worship services.

"O Store Gud" might have continued to have been sung by only a few eastern European and Swedish Christians if Hitler had not invaded Poland. With Nazis bent on controlling all of Europe, Hine was forced to return to England. He brought "O Store Gud" with him but did not attempt to get it published.

It was almost a decade later, in 1948 while witnessing at a refugee camp filled with hundreds of Russians fleeing communism, that the old song jumped back into the missionary's mind. On that day Hine observed two men sharing the way to salvation with others in the Sussex, England, compound. The missionary intently listened as the Christian duo spoke of the awesome power of God. As if frozen, Hine continued to watch the men in much the same way Boberg must have observed the thunderstorm in Sweden.

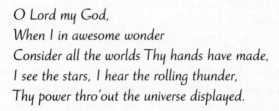

O Lord my God,
When I in awesome wonder
Consider all the worlds Thy hands have made,
I see the stars, I hear the rolling thunder,
Thy power thro'out the universe displayed.

Chorus:
Then sings my soul, my Savior God, to Thee;
How great Thou art, how great Thou art!
Then sings my soul, my Savior God, to Thee:
How great Thou art, how great Thou art!

When thro' the woods and forest glades I wander
And hear the birds sing sweetly in the trees,
When I look down from lofty mountain grandeur,
and hear the brook and feel the gentle breeze.

Chorus

And when I think that God,
His Son not sparing, sent Him to die,
I scarce can take it in,
That on the cross, my burdens gladly bearing,
He bled and died to take away my sin.

Chorus

When Christ shall come
With shout of acclamation
And take me home, what joy shall fill my heart!
Then I shall bow in humble adoration,
And there proclaim, my God, how great Thou art.

Chorus

When he finally tore himself away and headed to his home, the missionary was literally overcome with joy. It was as if he had felt the hand of God and it had opened his eyes, allowing him to see the love of Jesus brought down to earth through the witness of two poor and almost destitute Russian men.

Like Boberg before him, Hine pulled out his pen and tried to put into words what he felt at that moment. The one inspired verse, telling of the second coming of Christ, that found its way onto paper that day matched perfectly those of "O Store Gud." Translating Boberg's nine original stanzas into English (though only two of the original verses are commonly sung today) and adding his own new verse at the end, Hine took the song he called "How Great Thou Art" to a small printer and had the hymn published in leaflet form. Hine then used these pieces of paper like Bible tracts, sharing "How Great Thou Art" with everyone he met through his ministry.

Within a year, George Beverly Shea, the noted soloist who appeared at Billy Graham crusades, was given one of Hine's leaflets. Shea was impressed with the song's message and took it to Graham. Both men felt that "How Great Thou Art" could be used in an upcoming service in Canada in which the evangelist would be preaching on the Lord's power to transform lives. After more than six decades, "How Great Thou Art" was about to have a remarkable debut. Who could have guessed that on this evening in the early 1950s, Carl Boberg's song would touch more hearts than even the great Rev. Billy Graham's sermon?

Over the course of the next twenty years, "How Great Thou Art" became the most popular Christian song in the world. It rose to this status almost as quickly as the thunderstorm that had inspired its message. Yet because it was introduced and found worldwide acceptance at Billy Graham crusades, the hymn was thought of as an American classic. It was so loved by those in the United States that it moved out of religious circles and into the mainstream. Hundreds of recording artists cut "How Great Thou Art," using it in secular concerts while embracing it with a pride and respect that normally was reserved for "The Star-Spangled Banner."

From the day Boberg first shared "O Store Gud" with his congregation to the moment George Beverly Shea sang it in Canada, the message of "How Great Thou Art" did not change. Yet in spite of the fact that two world wars shook the foundation of the earth, dealing out death and destruction in a fashion never before witnessed, no one, not even Hine, realized the full power of the hymn. It took the advent of the nuclear age, a time when the whole world could be destroyed in an instant by the whim of a single man, for a spiritual revival to sweep across America and then around the world. In these days of insecurity, a song like "How Great Thou Art" brought hope and comfort. It was as if Boberg had been given the inspiration for the song not as much for his own time but for the time beginning with the cold war.

Another possible reason that "How Great Thou Art" swept the U.S. by storm in the fifties was the need for Americans to somehow set their country's ideals apart from those of the communist block. Boberg's hymn thus became a musical testimony of many Americans' belief that the power Christians found in worship would ultimately save the nation and its way of life while also dooming all those who refused to acknowledge the Lord's power and majesty. It is probably no coincidence that "How Great Thou Art" became the most popular inspirational song in the United States at the same time that "under God" was inserted into the Pledge of Allegiance in 1954.

Every time America is challenged, tens of millions are reminded of the song and cling to the message found in the words of "How Great Thou Art." This message, that God is greater than any other power in the world, has inspired the U.S. through wars and probably inspired Americans to attempt countless humanitarian missions of peace and compassion.

Remarkably, between the sudden 1880 downpour witnessed by a Swedish pastor and the introduction of this gospel classic to the world at a huge Billy Graham crusade sixty years later, the song was rarely sung outside of small churches. It was as if this great hymn could not be recognized until it was really needed. The spotlight finally shown on the magnificent anthem at the very moment in time when it had the power to calm the fears of a troubled world. "How Great Thou Art" now seems as American as the flag, hot dogs, and apple pie. In truth, to millions of Americans, it means much more than all of those icons combined.

I Love Thy Kingdom, Lord

On the eve of the most important battle his young country had ever faced, the commander of the Army of the Revolution looked haggard and worn. He had just walked through the cold wind and blowing snow to review his troops. His men's uniforms were tattered and torn, many soldiers were injured, and all were homesick. On several occasions the general had stopped and visited with some of the soldiers one-on-one. Though they acted brave and assured him they were ready to fight, their bravado couldn't hide what was so very obvious. The leader knew that in reality they were hungry, tired, and demoralized. He also realized these soldiers were aware that the well-trained and fully outfitted enemy seemed invincible, so they were scared too.

In spite of overwhelming odds, however, these men pledged that they were willing to give their lives for the cause of freedom. Though the experienced military veteran had served with much better trained soldiers than these quickly converted shopkeepers and farmers, he doubted he had ever known better men. For this reason they were like sons and brothers to him, and it was so hard to send them out to perhaps die on a battlefield. If the war was lost, then would their deaths be in vain? This question haunted George Washington until the final days of the war.

After his trek through the bleak winter night, the man who would ultimately be called the Father of Our Country sat down at the table in his tiny headquarters. Washington had risked everything he owned and held dear to lead this fight. At this moment it looked as though he had made the wrong choice. While he may have seemed invincible to his own Colonial troops, while he may have towered over all his soldiers, he also shared the doubts of the men who fought with him. At times, like tonight, even the legendary Washington wondered if the mighty British could ever be beaten.

Carrying such a burden of responsibility on this cold evening, the tall man from Mount Vernon sent word that he needed the counsel of his dear friend and personal chaplain, Timothy Dwight. Though his role is rarely mentioned in history books, Dwight was a mighty source of inspiration for the men who fought the long war for American independence. His words and his presence just might have been one of the most important secret weapons the Colonial army had.

The chaplain was a remarkable man, destined for an equally remarkable legacy. Each time Dwight met with Washington, the clergyman provided more than simple words or a prayer. Though still in his twenties, the young preacher seemed to exude an air of confidence and faith that always restored Washington's hope for victory and undergirded his belief that the cause for which he had volunteered was indeed just.

Washington put such great store in his chaplain's abilities to inspire that he regularly sent Dwight out to speak to the troops. Besides giving messages of hope and faith, the chaplain also wrote songs for the Continental army to use during religious services or when marching. These songs, now largely forgotten, combined patriotism and Christian

I love Thy kingdom, Lord,
The house of Thine abode,
The Church our blest Redeemer saved
With His own precious blood.

I love Thy Church, O God:
Her walls before Thee stand,
Dear as the apple of Thine eye,
And graven on Thy hand.

For her my tears shall fall;
For her my prayers ascend;
To her my cares and toils be given,
Till toils and cares shall end.

Beyond my highest joy
I prize her heavenly ways,
Her sweet communion, solemn vows,
Her hymns of love and praise.

Jesus, Thou friend divine,
Our Savior and our King,
Thy hand from every snare and foe
Shall deliverance bring.

Sure as Thy truth shall last,
To Zion shall be given
The brightest glories earth can yield,
And brighter bliss of heaven.

faith in a way that encouraged the soldiers to believe God was with them as they fought for independence. In the midst of great battles, many men died with the words of Dwight's songs on their lips and the gentle preacher holding their hand. Yet even as he watched young men die, the chaplain's belief in the cause of American freedom did not waver. Because of his attitude and steadfast belief in the cause, Dwight seemed an ideal pick for the position he held.

There were many critics who questioned why the general had not selected a much more experienced pastor to lend spiritual guidance to the troops. Some believed Dwight had been chosen as chaplain because he was Washington's close friend, and this was the case. Yet Washington picked the preacher not out of friendship but because of how impressed he was with the young man's intellect, faith, and speaking ability.

A grandson of one of early America's most remarkable theologians, Dwight was born in 1752 in Northampton, Massachusetts. By the age of four the boy had read most of the Bible. Within two years he was writing papers examining religious beliefs. At the age of thirteen he was a freshman at Yale, four years later becoming one of the famed university's youngest graduates. He then preached in Congregationalist churches where his messages astounded and inspired some of the future leaders of the United States. He met Washington in his role as pastor, and in 1776, after much prayer, Dwight joined his friend in America's fight for freedom.

Throughout the war, Dwight served at Washington's side. Besides praying with the general, the chaplain also sang to him. Though he did not publish any of his hymns of faith at the time, a host of those who won the battle for freedom either heard Dwight sing his compositions or heard Washington speak of what they had come to mean to him. The one message the young chaplain constantly drove home to both the general and his troops was that God's Spirit was with them and by the Lord's hand they would be delivered. This was a battle like David's with Goliath, Dwight often told Washington, and just like in the Bible, David would beat the giant. When the colonies finally saw the mighty British Empire surrender at Yorktown, Dwight's faith was realized.

There is little doubt that because of his role in supporting Washington throughout the war, the chaplain could have stayed with the general as he became the nation's first president. Yet the preacher accepted a different call, maybe one that was even more challenging than providing spiritual leadership for the newly formed United States of America.

Dwight, whose passions were preaching, writing, and education, left the army and founded the nation's first seminary, Andover. After leading this new school and pastoring in Connecticut, he accepted the position as president of Yale in 1795. When he took the reins at the famous Ivy League institution, there was only one member of the student body who claimed to be a practicing Christian, but under Dwight's guidance a revival began. Within five years the university became one of the most important centers of faith and inspiration in the New World.

Around 1800 bodily weakness, caused by a near fatal bout with smallpox and compounded by vision problems and severe headaches, began to plague Dwight. Though still two years short of fifty, the man now looked much older than those who had served with him during the Revolution. His duties at Yale took every bit of the energy he had, and yet the pain he suffered allowed him very little rest. Nevertheless, when he was asked to write a hymnbook for Americans, a book filled with inspiration for those in this brave new world, Dwight again answered his nation's call to duty.

Dwight had been studying the book of Psalms when, with his head pounding and his vision blurred, he was given an inspiration about his place in the Lord's kingdom. Though he could barely see the paper and had to take constant breaks just to cradle his throbbing head in his hands, Dwight would not give up until he had finished the verses of his new song. The words that found their way onto the paper that day were very similar to those he had once shared with Washington during a time of war. Matching these lyrics to an existing tune, Dwight's "I Love Thy Kingdom, Lord" became the anchor for his hymnbook, *Psalms of David*.

"I Love Thy Kingdom, Lord" quickly established itself as one of the most popular hymns in the United States. Some of the founding fathers and early leaders of the country not only requested this song at church services but also sang it with great energy at almost every public event. They sang it as much as a tribute to the man as they did for the hymn's great message. America's early leaders knew Timothy Dwight not only as a brilliant educator but also as one of the strongest anchors of faith in America. They realized this preacher had played a mighty role in the freedom each of them cherished so dearly and were now entrusted to preserve. In the eyes of the legends of the fight for liberty, Dwight was more than just a friend and spiritual advisor; he represented early America's faith, courage, and Christian convictions. His mere presence in a room always reminded others that God was alive and vitally interested in their day-to-day lives.

Though suffering greater pain and more blindness each year, Timothy Dwight continued to lead Yale until his death in 1817. When news of his passing reached the nation's newspapers, he was mourned not just at the university he had guided for decades but by the whole country. In Washington and scores of other cities, Americans fittingly paid tribute to the Chaplain of the Revolution by singing "I Love Thy Kingdom, Lord." And certainly the preacher did love God's kingdom even more than he loved the country whose freedom he had helped win.

"I Love Thy Kingdom, Lord" was the first great American hymn and is the oldest still sung in this country. It can be found in almost every denominational hymnal. Even though his song remains familiar to millions of Christians, Timothy Dwight is not remembered by many today. That would not bother the preacher, however, as Dwight had no desire to make history, just to be a part of it. His focus was on spreading the message of hope and faith to a struggling new nation. Timothy Dwight would probably be pleased to know that through his "I Love Thy Kingdom, Lord," that message is still being shared today in an America that has become the most powerful nation on earth. It has been more than two centuries since he stood by Washington's side, but the two great loves of Dwight's life, Christ and America, are still shining brightly in the world.

IT IS WELL WITH MY SOUL

uring moments of great pain and doubt, American Christians have turned to the words of Horatio G. Spafford to give them the strength and the faith to move forward. The inspirational song that has been such a blessing to so many was written not during a time of great thanksgiving and celebration but at the darkest period of this man's life. In just two years he had gone from the highest plane of emotional, spiritual, financial, and physical satisfaction to Job-like depths. Yet amazingly, his faith did not waver. Because of the way Spafford addressed the most crushing moment of his life, millions have been able to find a light in the darkness.

Spafford was born in North Troy, New York, on October 20, 1828. Blessed with a spirit of adventure, as a young adult he moved west, finally settling in Chicago. After passing the bar exam, Spafford quickly emerged not only as one of the Windy City's best attorneys but as a businessman who seemed to always be one step ahead of the competition. Sensing the city would grow into a mecca for commerce and industry, Spafford invested heavily in real estate along Lake Michigan. Initially this move enhanced his wealth and his position in the community. Ultimately, however, the venture marked the first in a series of disasters that would literally bring the man to his knees.

Besides work, Spafford had two other great loves. One was his family, consisting of his loving wife and their four daughters, Tanetta, Maggie, Annie, and Bessie. The other was his dedication to Christian missions. Spafford devoted a great deal of extra hours to Presbyterian lay work. He gave his time and money to foreign missions, revivals, food kitchens, and street ministries. The businessman was also one of the guiding forces behind the building of the first YMCA in the world. Because of his faithful stewardship and Christian leadership, Spafford's friends included the greatest evangelical ministers of the era—Dwight L. Moody, Ira David Sankey, and Philip Bliss. He worked with these men in their revival campaigns and helped shape the nature of their outreach.

In 1871 Spafford was sitting on top of the world. Every investment he had made had paid off, his church work had become just as rewarding as his business successes, the city looked upon him as one of their greatest leaders, and his family was healthy and happy. Spafford continually told his friends that he had been blessed beyond measure. He could never have imagined that a humble farm animal would set in motion an event that in the span of a few short hours took almost all his material wealth.

When Mrs. O'Leary's cow knocked over a lantern, a fire started in a barn that would burn much of the city of Chicago. Horatio Spafford's business holdings turned to ash before his eyes. By the end of the long night, about all the man had left from his business empire was his law degree. Everything else had gone up in smoke.

Spafford's financial fall hit his wife hardest of all. It broke her heart to see her husband lose a lifetime of work in just a few hours. Even as he was regrouping and starting to rebuild, she was falling apart. Her health deteriorated so rapidly that the family doctor suggested Spafford take her on a lengthy vacation. The physician felt time away from the worries that plagued her in Chicago might help restore her spirit.

After getting his business problems in order, Spafford arranged for an extended family trip to Europe. Seeing the Old World would fulfill a lifelong dream for his wife, and it would also give him a chance to team up with Moody and Sankey during their London crusade. The Spaffords traveled by train to New York. It was an exciting trip during which the family eagerly planned what they wanted to see on the other side of the Atlantic. But just before they were scheduled to depart America, Horatio was notified of a business problem in Chicago. Rather than take his wife and daughters back to the Windy City, he took them to the dock and watched them embark on the SS *Ville du Havre*, assuring them he would catch up with them in France by Christmas. With one less passenger in the party, Spafford even managed to arrange for the family to change cabins, moving them up to nicer accommodations in the bow. Though it seemed to be in their best interest at the time, the move would prove to be fatal.

On November 22, Spafford had just about taken care of the business problems in Chicago. If all went well, he figured he could leave for New York during the first week in December. At that same time, halfway across the Atlantic his family was having the time of their lives. The ocean crossing had been beautiful so far, and Mrs. Spafford's

When peace, like a river, attendeth my way,
When sorrows like sea-billows roll;
Whatever my lot, Thou hast taught me to say,
It is well, it is well with my soul.

Chorus:
It is well with my soul,
It is well, it is well with my soul.

Though Satan should buffet, tho' trials should come,
Let this blest assurance control,
That Christ has regarded my helpless estate,
And hath shed His own blood for my soul.

Chorus

My sin — oh, the bliss of this glorious thought,
My sin — not in part but the whole,
Is nailed to the cross and I bear it no more,
Praise the Lord, praise the Lord, O my soul!

Chorus

For me, be it Christ, be it Christ hence to live:
If Jordan above me shall roll,
No pang shall be mine, for in death as in life
Thou wilt whisper Thy peace to my soul.

Chorus

But, Lord, 'tis for Thee, for Thy coming we wait,
The sky, not the grave, is our goal;
Oh trump of the angel! Oh voice of the Lord!
Blessed hope, blessed rest of my soul!

Chorus

And Lord, haste the day when the faith shall be sight,
The clouds be rolled back as a scroll,
The trump shall resound and the Lord shall descend,
"Even so" — it is well with my soul.

Chorus

health had already improved. The girls were so excited they could barely stay still. To each of them the trip was like a fairy tale come true.

Somehow, in the middle of the huge ocean, the SS *Ville du Havre* strayed into the path of a western-bound British ship. With both vessels traveling at full speed, the impact was crushing. The *Ville du Havre* was almost cut in half at the bow, and passengers and baggage were literally tossed off the decks into the water. In just twelve minutes the *Ville du Havre* sank, carrying 226 to the bottom of the ocean.

News of the shipwreck reached the U.S. before any of the survivors made land in England. Thus hundreds of anxious families were forced to wait prayerfully to hear if their loved ones had somehow escaped with their lives. One of those praying for good news was Horatio Spafford. Seven days after the accident, on December 1, when the survivors landed at Cardiff, Wales, Mrs. Spafford sent a telegram to her husband in Chicago. There were just two words on the communiqué: "Saved alone." The proud parents of four were now childless.

Spafford wired his wife to wait in England for him, promising that he would catch the next ship headed east. Rushing to New York, the lawyer booked passage on the first ship bound for England. As the voyage began,

Spafford braved the cold winter wind and walked to a spot near the vessel's bow, staring out across the water. He kept watch at that position for most of the trip.

It was while standing at the ship's rail that the words of his friend, Dwight Moody, came back to the grieving man. One of the evangelist's most famous quotes might well have done more than lift Spafford's spirits at that moment; it might just have inspired him to compose a poem that became his most public legacy of faith.

Moody had once told thousands at revival meetings, "Someday you will read in the papers that D. L. Moody of East Northfield is dead. Don't you believe a word of it! At that moment I shall be more alive than I am now; I shall have gone up higher, that is all, out of this old clay tenement into a house that is immortal—a body that death cannot touch, that sin cannot taint; a body fashioned like unto His glorious body."

As Spafford considered the reality of death and the surety of his faith, he began to realize that his daughters were very much alive. He would not see them again for a while, but they were now better off than any of those on the ship around him. As this thought welled up in his soul, the captain of the ship called out to him, "Mr. Spafford, we are nearing the spot where your daughters now rest."

The downcast father suddenly felt the girls' spirits around him. Rather than cry, he smiled. He was flooded with a sense of peace. For the first time in more than a week, he felt the Lord's hand on his shoulder.

Rushing to his cabin, Spafford picked up pen and paper and quickly jotted down the words that were suddenly on his heart:

> When peace, like a river, attendeth my way,
> When sorrows like sea-billows roll;
> Whatever my lot, Thou hast taught me to say,
> It is well, it is well with my soul.

The poem that was inspired by passing near his daughters' watery graves brought much comfort to Spafford and his wife. When they returned to Chicago and were surrounded by friends and family, the lawyer shared the poem with them as well. His inspired words assured them all that things were going to be all right.

One of those who came by to help comfort the Spaffords was their close friend Philip Bliss. Bliss was a vocalist and songwriter who worked with some of the greatest names in early American music. As Bliss listened to Spafford's poem, he was deeply moved. The songwriter made a copy for himself. At his home Bliss composed music for the poem, creating a song he called "It Is Well with My Soul." Within weeks he was singing the new hymn at Moody's crusades. It quickly became one of the most requested songs at the revival meetings.

Though Horatio Spafford managed to rebuild a great deal of his personal wealth over the next decade, he ultimately gave it up. He felt a need to go to the Holy Land. Once there, he and his wife founded a ministry called American Colony. Reaching out to the poor, the Spaffords saved thousands of lives each year by feeding the hungry and treating the sick.

Their ministry was so strong and meant so much to the region that it continued long after their deaths.

Yet as meaningful as was Spafford's outreach in the Holy Land, it could not come close to the impact of the thoughts he set to music during the darkest days of his life. "It Is Well with My Soul" is an American gift of faith that has inspired millions around the world. It has helped people through wars, disasters, and heartbreak. It has encouraged countless souls to not give up but to go on. Every time America has needed an anthem that addresses pain that seems too deep to bear, "It Is Well with My Soul" has come to the forefront. While the hymn may not cause the chest to swell in pride like "America, the Beautiful" or bring patriotic joy like "God Bless America," it has become the principle reminder of faith for millions during times of tribulation. And like America, "It Is Well with My Soul" has stood the test of time.

JESUS LOVES ME

*T*aken from the pages of a best-selling novel and inspired by the prospect of an American Civil War, "Jesus Loves Me" might well be the best-known song in the history of the Christian church. Ironically, the circumstances that led to the birth of the simple children's hymn began not out of a desire to create a new song but rather out of the need of two sisters to find a way to make ends meet after the death of their father. Little did they realize that a poem from one page in one book would be transformed into a statement of faith for children and adults around the globe.

Anna and Susan Warner were a rarity in early America. Because of family financial security and a progressive-minded father, the sisters were highly educated at a time when schools were closed to many females. Motherless since childhood, Anna and Susan were the focal points of their father's life. The three became so close that the sisters never left the home where they were born, living their whole lives near the U.S. Military Academy at West Point. Mr. Warner was one of New York City's most prominent attorneys, so the sisters had few responsibilities and no real worries. Throughout the early and mid-1850s, they spent their spare time teaching Sunday school at West Point and doing volunteer work in the local community. If a double tragedy had not invaded their lives, Anna and Susan would probably have lived and died in relative obscurity.

A national economic depression wiped out the Warner family investments in 1857. Their father, his spirit broken by the collapse of his holdings, never fully recovered. Mr. Warner died not long after losing everything he owned besides the family home. In order to eat and pay bills, the Warner sisters used their substantial education. Discovering they had a flair for composing fiction, the women quickly found a publisher and scored an overnight best-seller with *The Wide, Wide World*. Other successful novels quickly followed. Yet while a number of these books rivaled *Uncle Tom's Cabin* in sales, none would have the worldwide influence as did one written by Anna, *Say and Seal*.

While it was a good read, the novel was not a work that would go down in history as being an important contribution to American literature. If not for one scene in which the lead character comforts a dying child, *Say and Seal* and Anna Warner would probably have been completely forgotten long ago. In a pivotal moment of the story, the kindly Mr. Linden comes to the bedside of Johnny Fax. The sick child looks up at Linden, searching his face for some kind of strength and hope. The man, overcome with grief, pats the boy as he softly recites a poem.

> *Jesus loves me! This I know,*
> *For the Bible tells me so.*
> *Little ones to Him belong;*
> *They are weak, but He is strong.*
>
> *Jesus loves me! He will stay*
> *Close beside me all the way;*
> *Thou hast died and bled for me,*
> *I will henceforth live for Thee.*
>
> *Jesus loves me! loves me still,*
> *Tho' I'm very weak and ill;*

That I might from sin be free,
Bled and died upon the tree.

Jesus loves me! He who died,
Heaven's gate to open wide;
He will wash away my sin,
Let His little child come in.

These are the last words Johnny ever hears and perhaps the most touching moment in the hundreds of pages of *Say and Seal.*

Warner's writings about trials and death, the love of Jesus, and the promise of everlasting life were really her personal testimony. She believed the four verses she put in the book as much as she believed anything. Yet her reason for interjecting them into her plot was probably inspired by the looming Civil War. She knew the South and North would surely come to blows over the issues of states' rights and slavery. She felt equally sure that many of the young men she had taught in Sunday school at West Point would die or be gravely injured during this war. Therefore, her verses were as much for each of the readers who would soon be facing death as they were for her imaginary Johnny Fax.

One of those who bought a copy of *Say and Seal* was Dr. William B. Bradbury, one of the most important forces in American church music. The middle-aged man from Maine had discovered, arranged, written, or published hundreds of hymns. His tireless hours perfecting and preserving early American gospel songs are still being felt today. Some of his greatest songs, such as "He Leadeth Me," "Sweet Hour of Prayer," and "The Solid Rock," have become some of the most powerful Christian songs found in hymnals.

Jesus loves me! This I know,
For the Bible tells me so.
Little ones to Him belong;
They are weak, but He is strong.

Chorus:
Yes, Jesus loves me! Yes, Jesus loves me!
Yes, Jesus loves me! The Bible tells me so.

Jesus loves me! loves me still,
Tho' I'm very weak and ill;
That I might from sin be free,
Bled and died upon the tree.

Chorus

Jesus loves me! He who died,
Heaven's gate to open wide;
He will wash away my sin,
Let His little child come in.

Chorus

Jesus loves me! He will stay
Close beside me all the way;
Thou hast bled and died for me,
I will henceforth live for Thee.

Chorus

On an evening in 1860, the great musician just wanted to escape from his work and music for a while by reading a good book. Yet in the pages of Warner's novel, Bradbury found inspiration unlike any he had ever known. As the songwriter read Linden's words to Johnny Fax, he did not think of the verses as a poem but rather as a song. Sitting down at his piano, he developed a simple melody to accompany Warner's words. Yet as he played through his final arrangement, it somehow felt incomplete. Picking up a pen, he quickly composed a chorus that was even more elementary than the words found in the original poem.

> Yes, Jesus loves me!
> Yes, Jesus loves me!
> Yes, Jesus loves me!
> The Bible tells me so.

This simple affirmation, actually little more than a restating of Warner's first verse, gave "Jesus Loves Me" a sense of completion. Playing the song again, Bradbury sensed that he had helped create something very special. With Warner's permission, he quickly published what he thought would become an important children's song. Little did he know it would be the most important hymn he would ever bring to the American people.

During the Civil War, "Jesus Loves Me" quickly spread across the battlefields. As very few battles took place after dark, soldiers usually gathered around campfires to share stories and sing songs. During these long evenings, "Jesus Loves Me" was often heard on both sides of the lines at the same time. Meanwhile, away from the battlefronts, children and adults were singing the new hymn in church, in school, and at community gatherings. During this four-year period of death and destruction, "Jesus Loves Me" even became America's most popular lullaby.

The Warner-Bradbury song might have first swept the nation due to a war, but in peace "Jesus Loves Me" went well beyond the confines of the United States. Missionaries took the song with them as they traveled overseas. It was often the first Christian song taught to adults and children in Africa, Asia, and South America. It has even been claimed that this American children's song has been responsible for more conversions than any Bible verse, sermon, or hymn. Inspired by one woman's desire to help a nation deal with the death and suffering of a war she knew was coming, put into a book as

a subtle way of sharing her own faith, Anna Warner's "Jesus Loves Me" became the greatest American missionary tool of all time.

As her song continues to lead men and women to Christ, Anna Warner's body rests in the soil of a uniquely American institution. The woman who gave the world "Jesus Loves Me" is buried on the grounds of the United States Military Academy at West Point. She is so honored because of her unflagging spiritual support of the army cadets.

15

JUST AS I AM

Perhaps no song better reflects and defines the marriage of the American Dream and Christian faith than "Just As I Am." Though America is never mentioned in its lyrics, for hundreds of millions around the world who have come to know Christ through the ministry of evangelist Dr. Billy Graham, the promise found in the United States and the promise found in Christianity fully come together in this hymn. It is hard for many to believe, therefore, that this American revival icon actually was written not by an American but by a housebound British woman whose search for meaning, purpose, and freedom never took her beyond her own bedroom.

As a youth, Charlotte Elliot had boundless energy. She was a dynamo who excelled as an artist and poet. Her laugh was almost as well known in Brighton, England, as was her wit. By 1800, when Miss Elliot turned twenty-one, she had emerged as one of the area's most talented and vibrant personalities. It seemed nothing could or would ever stop her. As her friends watched her almost skip through each duty and activity, none would have guessed that her carefree days were numbered. Within nine years she would find herself confined to her bed, the world that she had so loved to personally greet each day off limits for the remainder of her life.

For Charlotte Elliot illness hit like lightning. One day she was literally running from friend to friend, laughter punctuating her every move, the next she was saddled with an unknown disease that weakened her to the point where walking across the room took all the energy she could muster. After sickness struck, she patiently waited weeks for a cure, but none came. Then for months she looked toward a death that did not come. Finally, after more than a year of being all but chained to her bed, hopeless and helpless, she lifted her voice and demanded to know how God could do this to her. That was the moment when all of the charm and creativity left Charlotte's soul. Depression and bitterness now not only registered in every word she spoke but also were etched in the cold, hard, hateful glare that constantly showed on her face. Her eyes, once filled with mischief and vitality, became dark and brooding. No one wanted to be around her for more than a few minutes at a time.

Elliot's brother, an Anglican minister, took the helpless Charlotte in, and a host of other local ministers came to visit and pray for the woman over the next decade. Yet nothing changed, not her health nor her attitude, and Charlotte fell into a deep, dark hole filled with bitterness and resentment. She spent most of her time thinking about what could have been. In her other waking hours she questioned why she continued to breathe when her life had no purpose and her once dynamic talents had withered away to nothing.

In 1822, noted Swiss evangelist Dr. Caesar Malan was on a speaking tour of England. At the request of Charlotte's brother, Malan paid a visit to the Elliot home. For a while the minister just sat by Charlotte's bed as she recounted her many woes. Finally, when he could take no more of her negative talk, Malan asked a simple question that cut to the root of the woman's real problem.

"Why do you think you were struck down?" Malan asked.

Charlotte quickly replied, "Because of something I did. I must have been a bad person. I must have sinned."

Malan then asked Charlotte to ask God for help and strength.

The woman shook her head and told the great preacher, "I am not worthy of having God help me."

Malan smiled and looked into the woman's face. "You are right to feel a sense of sin," he said. "Without it no one comes to the Savior for pardon and new life."

Charlotte considered the man's words, then shot back with a challenge of her own.

"What have I got to offer Christ?"

Malan answered, "You have nothing of merit to bring to God. None of us does. He does not really need anything we have. He just wants you as you are, a sinner."

With this new concept in mind, Charlotte accepted Christ as her Savior on that day. Becoming a Christian did not end her suffering, return her energy and health, or allow her to leave her bed, but it did give her a new spirit and outlook. She began to smile, laugh, and write again. She also now searched for ways to lift the spirits of those who came to her bedside. For the next forty-nine years she continued this practice and personally touched thousands with her warmth and kind words.

In Brighton, Elliot once again became an inspiration. Yet it was a dozen years after she was saved that Charlotte, inspired by her own spiritual experience, penned the words to the hymn that has invited thousands to a personal relationship

Just as I am, without one plea,
But that Thy blood was shed for me,
And that Thou bidd'st me come to Thee,
O Lamb of God, I come! I come!

Just as I am, and waiting not
To rid my soul of one dark blot,
To Thee whose blood can cleanse each spot,
O Lamb of God, I come! I come!

Just as I am, though tossed about
With many a conflict, many a doubt,
Fightings and fears within, without,
O Lamb of God, I come! I come!

Just as I am, poor, wretched, blind;
Sight, riches, healing of the mind,
Yea, all I need in Thee to find,
O Lamb of God, I come! I come!

Just as I am, Thou wilt receive,
Wilt welcome, pardon, cleanse, relieve,
Because Thy promise I believe,
O Lamb of God, I come! I come!

Just as I am, Thy love unknown
Hath broken ev'ry barrier down
Now to be Thine, yea, Thine alone,
O Lamb of God, I come! I come!

with Christ. Charlotte wrote hundreds of hymns, yet the one that became the best known and most treasured was inspired by her own search for a way to serve Christ. When she considered the vast needs of the world and her own inability to get out of bed and meet those needs, she was overwhelmed with a sense of impotency.

"God knows me well," she explained to her brother. "He knows what it is, day after day, hour after hour, to fight against the bodily feelings of almost overpowering weakness, languor, and exhaustion, to resolve not to yield to slothfulness, depression, and stability such as the body causes me to long to indulge, but to rise every morning determined to take my motto: 'If a man will come after me, let him deny himself, take up his cross and follow me.' God sees, God guards, and God guides me. His grace surrounds me, and his voice continually bids me to be happy and holy in his service, just where I am."

Seizing upon that concept, Charlotte quickly wrote the first three verses to "Just As I Am." To Charlotte it was a very personal song, a testimony not meant for other eyes but to be used as a reminder that God loved her no matter how little she had to give back to him. It was her way of reinforcing that when it came to salvation,

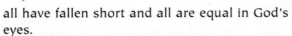

all have fallen short and all are equal in God's eyes.

With her permission, Charlotte's brother printed "Just As I Am" and used it during his services. Soon the song was published in an English hymnal. As more and more churches adopted the hymn, ministers discovered that even though the message in each line was really Charlotte's life story, almost everyone in their congregations could strongly identify with the message found in Elliot's words. By 1850 the song had been used all over Britain and had crossed the Atlantic, where it was quickly adopted by hundreds of American churches.

While "Just As I Am" became popular during the Civil War, it was the evangelist Billy Sunday who gave the English hymn its ultimate central purpose, as an altar call or song of invitation for salvation. Beginning in the 1940s, when America's Protestant revival torch was passed to Billy Graham, "Just As I Am" become the primary musical vehicle that transported spiritual seekers from their seats to the altar. Christ might have touched their hearts through a minister's message to bring about salvation, but it was "Just As I Am" that served as the usher to forgiveness and the cross.

Rev. Graham soon took his crusades around the world, speaking before millions in every corner of the globe. At each stop, in each place where Christ was offered to the world's sinners, "Just As I Am" was played and sung. Thus, there can be little doubt that Graham's incredible revival meetings paved the way for an invalid English woman's testimony to become known as an American institution and a beacon of Christian faith. Thanks to the fact that Billy Graham represented America to millions around the globe, the song's message took on two unique meanings. To the poor, oppressed, and imprisoned, "Just As I Am" reflected both the path to salvation and the special blessings that being an American offered to those fortunate to call it home. Therefore, "Just As I Am" became a song about spiritual and literal freedom for many.

In New York harbor, towering almost three hundred feet above the water, stands the famous symbol of freedom, hope, and security—the Statue of Liberty. Created by a Frenchman and given to the United States in honor of the nation's first hundred years of democracy, this sculpture trumpets the fact that the United States has accepted countless immigrants from around the world "just as they are." Inscribed on the Statue of Liberty are words that seem to echo God's own call to his people.

> Give me your tired, your poor,
> Your huddled masses yearning to breathe free,
> The wretched refuse of your teeming shore.
> Send these, the homeless, tempest-tost to me,
> I lift my lamp beside the golden door!

Charlotte Elliot never saw the United States. In her long life she saw little but the walls that surrounded her bed. Yet this woman came to understand a concept that makes Christian faith so unique and wonderful. "Just As I Am" is the way God made us, the way he sent us into this world, and the way we must come back to him. This message born in England has been taken to the whole world by Christian Americans.

MY COUNTRY, 'TIS OF THEE
(AMERICA)

s a college student, Oliver Wendell Holmes wrote a whimsical poem about his Harvard classmate, Samuel Francis Smith.

And there's a fine youngster of excellent pith,
Fate tried to conceal him by naming him Smith.

Smith, born in Newton Centre, Massachusetts, in 1808, was a bright young man of uncommon talent who probably could have risen to the top in any field he chose. But the creative boy from a small town had but one goal: to share the gospel with those who didn't know Christ and to expand the faith of those who did. So he ignored those who urged him to go into politics and business, instead accepting the call to preach. This decision set in motion a series of events that would give the United States its most blatantly Christian anthem and create a musical identity for this country that still rings true today.

After completing his degree at Harvard, Smith decided to continue his biblical training. With his intellect and educational background, he could have gone to Europe for study, but he decided to remain in America and pursue a theology degree at Andover Seminary in Newton Centre, Massachusetts.

In 1832 when Smith was in the middle of his studies, one of Smith's friends and mentors, William Woolbridge, spent his summer visiting Germany to see the sights and expand his knowledge of the European religious experience. When he returned to the United States, Woolbridge sought out Smith to share with him the wonders of what he had seen and heard. Smith listened with interest as Woolbridge told of unique worship services, incredible cathedrals, and musical anthems that seemed to come from heaven. Then Woolbridge brought out a trunk filled with German song-books. He insisted that in these pages were some of the greatest spiritual gems the world had ever been given. Yet Smith was not to be the first one allowed a chance to explore this musical treasure trove. Woolbridge had reserved that right for his close friend and New England's leading Christian publisher, Lowel Mason.

Mason, whose library was already filled with thousands of similar volumes from a number of different countries, grudgingly accepted Woolbridge's gift but spent little time thumbing through the volumes. The music he did review did not move him. As the gifted publisher and musician neither read nor spoke German, the text did nothing for him either. Like Woolbridge, Mason knew Samuel Smith, and he realized the student had a working knowledge of the German language. So Mason boxed up the materials and passed them on to the younger man, figuring he might have more time to study them and recommend materials worthy of performance or publication.

Unlike Mason and Smith, William Woolbridge was a musical amateur who might have been wowed by the German performances he heard. His musical friends didn't share his enthusiasm over the music when they read it on the page. Like Mason, on initial review Smith found little that moved him in the old songbooks. The formal feel of the

My country, 'tis of thee,
Sweet land of liberty,
Of thee I sing:
Land where my fathers died,
Land of the pilgrim's pride,
From every mountain side
Let freedom ring!

My native country, thee,
Land of the noble free,
Thy name I love:
I love thy rocks and rills,
Thy woods and templed hills;
My heart with rapture thrills
Like that above.

Let music swell the breeze,
And ring from all the trees
Sweet freedom's song:
Let mortal tongues awake;
Let all that breathe partake;
Let rocks their silence break,
The sound prolong.

Our father's God, to Thee,
Author of liberty,
To Thee we sing:
Long may our land be bright
With freedom's holy light;
Protect us by Thy might,
Great God, our King!

German hymns left him somewhat cold. The student felt American music had much more life and energy. Still, because he had promised Mason to at least look at each of the songs, he devoted a cold winter afternoon to their study.

Spreading the books out on a table, Smith leafed through a few pages of the first one he picked up and quickly grew bored. But just about the time he was going to give up and rebox the volumes, he came across a melody that interested him. It was vastly different from the gothic selections he had already dismissed. This tune was simple, straightforward, and had a New World feel to it. After humming the melody a few times, Smith glanced down and translated the German lyrics into English.

> *God save our gracious Queen*
> *Long live our noble Queen,*
> *God save the Queen!*
> *Send her victorious,*
> *happy and glorious,*
> *long to reign over us:*
> *God save the Queen!*

Smith wondered why this song had been placed in a hymnal. It did not appear to have been written to bring souls to Christ or strengthen faith. Rather, this was a patriotic ode asking the Lord to bless German rulers. Smith immediately felt he could create better lyrics than the Germans had composed for what Smith considered an inspired melody. The Germans might have hung everything on their leader's rule, but Smith knew Americans hung the

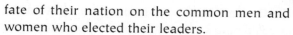

fate of their nation on the common men and women who elected their leaders.

Grabbing a pen and a scrap of paper, Smith looked out at the cold gray sky and began to search for inspiration that could carry the old tune in a new and more dramatic direction. Within half an hour he had written the lyrics of a new religious-patriotic anthem he called "America." Though he could not recall what prompted his theme, Smith later thought it might have simply been his feeling of love for his own country.

Smith was so excited by what he had just composed that he picked up his coat and hat and ventured out into the cold afternoon in search of his friends Mason and Woolbridge. When he played the song for them, the trio agreed that it spoke to what America really was. Concerned that a ruling class might yet take over America, the men were galvanized by a song that wasn't about George Washington or Thomas Jefferson or any king or queen; rather, "America" spoke of the nation and what it meant to the people.

Mason decided the new song needed to be arranged for multipart chorus vocals and taught to a children's choir. He thought voices that had been blessed by being born on American soil should give this gift to their country. A few months later on July 4, 1832, at the Park Street Church in Boston, "America" made its debut. The voices of five hundred children singing in front of a crowd of thousands brought the new song to life on that Declaration Day (now called Independence Day).

Smith was not just proud but awed by the power of the words he had been given. As he listened he honestly believed the German music had been written just so the United States could have an anthem of power, conviction, and faith. He thanked God for being given the opportunity to give those words to the world.

While Smith reveled in the glory of the moment, a number of those in the audience groaned. These folks knew the tune as the English national anthem, "God Save the Queen." As anti-British sentiments still ran very deep in the United States, some in the audience dismissed Smith's work out of hand, even declaring it blasphemous to connect anything American to anything English. It seemed that "America" might have been destined for only one performance.

"I wrote the hymn to suit the meter," Smith later explained. "It was the meter that instantly appealed to me. I was not too versed in non-American music and was therefore completely taken by surprise later when I was accused of being pro-British because I had used the tune."

Smith had never heard "God Save the Queen," nor had the majority of Americans of that era. Smith also didn't know that this tune he thought he had discovered had already been published in the United States with lyrics entitled "God Save the President" and "God Save George Washington." Though the English claimed that Henry Carey had written the music in 1715, the song was probably not of British origin. As a matter of fact, the Germans could not claim the tune either. The New York Sun, a prominent American newspaper in the 1800s, reported that the melody had once been used for the Prussian national anthem. Spain, Norway, and Finland had also used it as their national songs before it was adopted in England. French nuns sang the tune; it was used in a song to salute Louis XIV; and the

Swiss used it in 1602 as their national anthem.
There is some sketchy evidence to indicate that the Huns
brought it to Europe from Asia in the fourth century, and
others claim it was used by Jews in the first centuries after
Christ's birth. So who really wrote it? No one knows for
sure. Nor can anyone really claim to have sole rights to the
music.

To have anyone believe he would have intentionally
matched his words to a British national song broke Smith's
heart. Yet while most men would have trashed their work
or looked for a new tune, Smith would not give up. He
believed that his song had been inspired by God, that the
Lord's hand had guided his when he penned the lyrics, and
that this marriage of music and words was meant to be. So
he published his arrangement and continued to distribute
it throughout New England.

After the fury initially caused by linking the words to the
tune of "God Save the Queen" finally died down, "America"
became an American favorite. This was probably due to the
fact that so many hymnals included the song. This act itself
was remarkable. Most religious songbooks of the period did
not even contain well-known spirituals or gospel music songs
because they were thought to be too crude or not divinely
inspired. For a patriotic-themed standard to be positioned
beside honored hymns such as "Rock of Ages" was almost
unheard of. Yet Smith's inspiring lyrics won over even those
who argued for complete separation of church and state.

The Civil War also created an atmosphere in which
spiritual versions of patriotism were embraced by all those
who wore the uniform of the Union. On the day the flag
was shot down at Fort Sumter, "America" was sung in

Washington and in churches all across the North. As a symbol of solidarity and strength, "America" continued to be sung in the North at flag raisings, funerals, church services, and government meetings throughout the remainder of the war. President Lincoln loved the song and asked for it often at state functions. When the union was preserved, "America" was unofficially adopted as the nation's anthem. For the last forty decades of the nineteenth century, "America" meant so much to those in the United States that it was treated as if it was sacred. In 1895 the Pope even requested a copy of "America" written in the Baptist minister's own hand. This manuscript still rests in the Vatican Library.

In 1899, three years after Smith had died, Col. Nicholas Smith (no relation) wrote of "America," "It is recognized the world over as a great national hymn—beautifully simple in its poetry, rich in its patriotic sentiment, and vigorous enough to reflect the ennobling spirit of true American liberty." In the book *Stories of Great National Songs*, Col. Smith summed up the true power of "America" like this: "The song is simplicity itself, and yet it is a curious fact that others more gifted in poetic faculty, and of greater minds than Dr. Smith, have tried their best to make a song which would be truly a national anthem, but no one except this plain, kindly and noble-hearted Baptist clergyman has come within a thousand miles of success."

Seven decades after Samuel Smith died, another Baptist preacher, Dr. Martin Luther King Jr., used "America" as inspiration. In his famous August 28, 1963, "I Have a Dream" speech, King echoed Smith's words and then added to them.

This will be the day when all of God's children will be able to sing with a new meaning, "My country, 'tis of thee, sweet land of liberty, of thee I sing. Land where my fathers died, land of the pilgrim's pride, from every mountainside, let freedom ring."

And if America is to be a great nation this must become true. So let freedom ring from the prodigious hilltops of New Hampshire. Let freedom ring from the mighty mountains of New York. Let freedom ring from the heightening Alleghenies of Pennsylvania! Let freedom ring from the snowcapped Rockies of Colorado! Let freedom ring from the curvaceous peaks of California! But not only that; let freedom ring from Stone Mountain of Georgia! Let freedom ring from Lookout Mountain of Tennessee! Let freedom ring from every hill and every molehill of Mississippi. From every mountainside, let freedom ring.

Smith's old classmate, Oliver Wendell Holmes, who became the great chief justice of the Supreme Court, also knew the power of the song. In his last year of life, Holmes wrote, "Now, there's Smith. His name will be honored by every school child in the land when I have been forgotten a hundred years. He wrote 'My Country 'tis of Thee.' If he had said, 'Our Country,' the hymn would not have been immortal, but that 'My' was a masterstroke. Every one who sings the hymn at once feels a personal ownership in this native land. The hymn will last as long as the country."

It can be argued that there is a great deal wrong with America, but what Samuel Smith wrote more than 170 years ago is still embraced by Americans today. This probably would not have suprised Smith at all!

NEARER, MY GOD, TO THEE

pril 14, 1912, was a dark and foreboding night, an evening that should have created apprehension in all seafarers. Yet for those who walked the finely crafted decks of the world's most luxurious ocean liner, there was no fear, no trepidation, no worry. Nothing, not even the devil himself, could stop the Titanic—or so boasted those who built her. She was the finest and safest ship to ever glide over salt water.

The danger appeared out of nowhere. Though it was large, it didn't seem menacing. This iceberg looked pretty much like dozens of others that littered the North Atlantic each spring. Yet this frozen mountain was somehow different. Its silent, serene beauty secretly entombed a spirit of death. As if on a mission, it moved slowly toward the British vessel, playing a game of chicken with a man-made mechanical marvel that seemed to stand above all natural law. As the titan of a ship plowed forward, the hunk of ice skimmed its thick metal side, dropping pieces of frozen water across the forward decks. Then, the floating mountain moved on, not bothering to stop and witness the tragic drama it had just set in motion.

At first there was no reaction from the passengers and crew. Except for a slight jarring, most of those on board did not even note the actual event. The crew took the news of the hit almost as casually as did the more than two thousand ignorant passengers. It was only when one of the engineers inspected the damage that the truth was revealed.

Thomas Andrews of Harland and Wolff found that the icy giant had concealed a sharp cold knife just under the water's surface. That frozen blade had inflicted a lethal wound to the pride of the Star Line Fleet. Hurrying to the captain, Andrews solemnly announced that the ship would sink within two hours. As there were only enough lifeboats for half of the people on board, those in charge immediately realized they were about to preside over the most terrible calamity in the history of sailing. Though all the concerned officers ultimately understood the *Titanic*'s inevitable fate, at that point none of them could have guessed that this tragic end would forever be associated with a song written by a doomed English actress.

Sarah Flower Adams had been dead more than seven decades before that fateful night in 1912. Yet just like the ship's passengers and crew, in a very real way she knew from experience the fragility of life, the anguish of unrealized hopes and dreams, and the uncertainty of each moment. And like many who anxiously awaited their fate on the *Titanic*, Sarah had come to realize that the separation between life and death was as unpredictable as the North Atlantic and as unforgiving as a cold wind. Adams also believed the only real security in this world was found not in man-made marvels, not in fame or money, but in Christian faith.

Born in Harlow, Essex, England, on February 22, 1805, Sarah Flower was both a beautiful and talented woman. Outgoing and well educated, her flair for drama paved the way for her debut appearance on the London stage while she was still a teen. Quickly recognized as one of Britain's brightest young stage actresses, her delicate features and strong voice made her a star when others her age were mere stand-ins. By eighteen she had charmed tens of thousands of theater patrons in a wide variety of dramatic vehicles. One of her adoring fans, William Bridges Adams, married Flower in 1834. The union of the successful businessman and the famed actress had all of London talking.

Adams fully supported his wife's career and in 1837, when she played Lady Macbeth at London's Richmond Theater, he was cheering the loudest. At that moment the new Mrs. Adams appeared to be unstoppable. Yet after this performance the unthinkable happened. The seemingly strong and vibrant actress was hit by a number of major health problems. In a matter of months she went from being one of England's most vital theatrical personalities to an all but housebound invalid. Though weakened and obviously living on borrowed time, Adams remained determined to find an outlet for her creative flair and make all of England again take note of her talent.

Sarah's father, Benjamin Flower, was one of Europe's best-known publishers. He had once edited the *Cambridge Intelligencer* and the *Political Review*. One of his daughters, Eliza, was a composer. The influence of both her father and sister no doubt inspired Sarah to write poetry and drama. When she had somewhat refined her skills, she teamed with Eliza and produced more than a dozen musical works that were used in scores of Anglican churches across Britain. Not

Nearer, my God, to Thee,
Nearer to Thee!
E'en though it be a cross
That raiseth me;
Still all my song shall be,
Nearer, my God, to Thee,
Nearer, my God, to Thee,
Nearer to Thee!

Though like a wanderer,
The sun gone down,
Darkness be over me,
My rest a stone;
Yet in my dreams I'd be
Nearer, my God, to Thee,
Nearer, my God, to Thee,
Nearer to Thee!

There let the way appear,
Steps unto heav'n;
All that Thou sendest me,
In mercy giv'n;
Angels to beckon me

Nearer, my God, to Thee,
Nearer, my God, to Thee,
Nearer to Thee!

Then, with my waking
    thoughts
Bright with Thy praise,
Out of my stony griefs,
Bethel I'll raise;
So by my woes to be
Nearer, my God, to Thee,
Nearer, my God, to Thee,
Nearer to Thee!

Or if on joyful wing
Cleaving the sky,
Sun, moon, and stars
    forgot,
Upward I fly,
Still all my song shall be,
Nearer, my God, to Thee,
Nearer, my God, to Thee,
Nearer to Thee!

suprisingly, Sarah's star had quickly risen again, and many of her old theater fans now had fallen in love with her music. Yet it was a request from an outside party that inspired Adams to produce the song that would comfort not just those on a doomed ocean liner but millions of others all around the world.

In 1840 Rev. William J. Fox was a well-respected London minister with a large and loyal congregation. Besides delivering some of the most quoted sermons of the era and writing well-received theological papers, he also published hymns. Knowing Sarah's talent, Fox asked her to create a new religious song, one that he could use with a sermon he had written on Jacob and Esau. After studying Genesis 28:10–22, Sarah quickly composed "Nearer, My God, to Thee."

The story of the biblical brothers and their troubled father can easily be recognized in the song's simple and straightforward lyrics. Yet the verses are probably more autobiographical than biblical. The cross that is noted in the first stanza had to have been inspired by Sarah's constant battle with illness and her early retirement from the craft she so dearly loved. As she was growing weaker each day, she also had to have believed that she was literally nearer to God and heaven with each breath she took. The pain and hope contained in each of the next verses must have represented her own struggles as well. Yet also clearly spelled out in each phrase was the woman's undying faith in her Lord and the fact that no matter what she faced, she felt him near her at all times.

Within months of its debut at the church where Adams often worshiped, "Nearer, My God, to Thee" was published. By 1848, when Sarah Flower Adams died at the age of thirty-four, thousands in England were familiar with the hymn. Yet it took the input of another writer to make the song a universal favorite on both sides of the Atlantic.

Lowell Mason was born in Orange, New Jersey, on July 8, 1792. A musical prodigy, as a teen he directed his church choir and taught at singing schools. Though obviously gifted and desperate to compose, Mason opted for a safer and more profitable life in business. This quest took him to Savannah, Georgia, in 1812, where he quickly established himself as a respected banker. Still he did not completely give up on music. With Handel as his influence, Mason began to write original scores. Yet when his work was rejected time and again, he essentially gave up, using his musical skills only in church.

Without Mason's knowledge, the Handel and Haydn Society of Massachusetts had discovered his rejected pieces, put them in book form, and published them. In the first few months after its release, the banker's songbook sold fifty thousand copies. When they finally located Mason, the Handel and Haydn Society convinced him to give up his career as a financial leader and return to New England to compose.

For the next twenty years Mason was one of the greatest movers and shakers in American Christian music. His original melodies were teamed with scores of inspirational songs including "My Faith Looks Up to Thee" and "Joy to the World." He taught and influenced hundreds of up-and-coming American writers. By 1845 he had established himself as one of the New World's most gifted composers, arrangers, and publishers.

A decade after Sarah Flower Adams's death, Mason stumbled onto "Nearer, My God, to Thee." He probably first came across the Englishwoman's work in *Disciples Hymn Book*, a collection of music that had been published by James Freeman Clark. At the time he initially encountered "Nearer, My God, to Thee," Mason was assembling a new songbook. He didn't like the English melody that accompanied Adams's lyrics, however, so he didn't feel moved to include this hymn in his upcoming project. Two friends, Edward Park and Austin Phelps, prevailed upon Mason to reconsider the hymn. They argued that the lyrics had real merit and that Mason could probably rework the tune into something that would measure up to Adams's incredible words. As he restudied the work that was relatively unknown in the United States, the English song began to haunt the American composer. Though there were elements in "Nearer, My God, to Thee" he did not like, he could not set it aside.

"The meter was irregular," he later said, explaining why the song did not initially impress him. "But one night, while lying awake in the dark, eyes wide open, through the stillness of the house the melody came to me, and the next morning I wrote down the notes to a tune I called 'Bethany.'" This marriage of a former actress's words and a retired banker's music was first published in 1859.

With its new tune, "Nearer, My God, to Thee" quickly became an American favorite. And two years later, when the Union was split and brothers were literally fighting brothers in a Civil War, the song took on a deeper meaning than either

Adams or Mason could have predicted. Troops on both sides sang "Nearer, My God, to Thee" before battles. It was heard in field hospitals, churches, and during hurriedly organized battlefront funerals. At a time when God's love often seemed millions of miles away, people everywhere clung to the song as if it were the only thread of Christian hope they could still find. Though Lee's surrender to Grant ended the battlefield suffering, "Nearer, My God, to Thee" remained a rallying cry of the American spirit. It was sung by thousands after the assassination of Lincoln and continued to be used for memorial services in the years just after the war. In 1872 during the Boston Peace Celebration, the Adams-Mason hymn was the musical centerpiece of the choral presentation. Four years later it was used in scores of centennial celebrations from coast to coast.

By 1900 many considered "Nearer, My God, to Thee" to be the classic American hymn. It seemed that everyone knew it, and millions called it their favorite religious song. So it was hardly surprising that when President McKinley was shot in 1901, he requested that the hymn be sung at his bedside. His friends and family bravely attempted to make it through the verses as the gravely wounded president mouthed the words with them. Newspapers across the world reported McKinley's final request, noting that "Nearer, My God, to Thee" had been the musical vehicle that had taken the popular leader to his final home.

As the *Titanic*'s midnight bell struck and April 14 became the fifteenth, panic seized passengers all over the ship. Though the crew attempted to enforce the age-old custom of women and children first, when the passengers discovered there were not enough lifeboats, the noble tradition lost favor. Fights broke out, people were pushed overboard, and many who should have been given a spot on a lifeboat were left behind. As the minutes passed and the ship began to list more in the water, death began to stalk every deck. In the chaos, hundreds of voices shouted, screamed, and cursed as men and women battled for one last chance at life.

Sensing that something had to be done to bring order to the scene, the *Titanic*'s orchestra assembled on the deck and began to play popular music. As the ship sunk deeper into the sea, contemporary music seemed out of place, and the men began to play old hymns instead. Their final choice was "Nearer, My God, to Thee." The musicians who made up the

Titanic's famed orchestra were probably familiar with McKinley's final request. They also probably knew that "Nearer, My God, to Thee" was one of the most popular funeral hymns in the United States. It was surely Adams's

message, more than the song's history, that paved the way for this doomed musical ensemble to employ that hymn to bring hope to a hopeless situation and faith to a moment when death was far more certain than life.

Initially the band just played the hymn as many of the fifteen hundred left on the ship cried and begged for help. Then, partway through the first verse, a few voices joined in. Within moments the yelling and screaming had all but stopped, replaced by hundreds singing as one the song that had been written by an actress who sensed she was very near to God and heaven. The lyrics were perfect for the moment. It was as if they had been written for this one time and for these dying people. For a few minutes on that cold and unforgiving night, one song hovered over the waves, somehow bringing a peace that would have seemed impossible. To those on the ship and in the water around the *Titanic,* the music became the Spirit of God, a vocal bridge between life and death, earth and heaven.

It has been called "a night to remember," but in truth it was a night that could never be forgotten. The world's greatest ship, the unsinkable monument to the power of modern engineering, was taken out by a mammoth hunk of ice. It was impossible for those who had put such great faith in man's work to comprehend. So the seven hundred who found a spot on one of the liner's few lifeboats must have watched in horror and disbelief as the music suddenly stopped and their friends and family were sucked into the cold salt water.

When the stories of those last moments reached New York and London, newspapers all over the world reported how the hymn had ushered two thousand souls into the next life. In the months that followed, churches in every corner of the globe played "Nearer, My God, to Thee" as a tribute to the greatest sea tragedy of the era.

Sarah Flower Adams's hymn did not go down with the *Titanic*, just like it was not stilled when the Civil War ended or President McKinley died. "Nearer, My God, to Thee" continued to inspire and bring hope in the wake of suffering and death during two world wars, a pair of Asian wars, and terrorist strikes on the United States in 2001. Why has this English song, now almost always matched to an American tune, meant so much to so many in the United States and around the world for so long? Probably because its message was inspired by the fact that we all share a common fate—death. If life had been fair, Sarah Flower Adams might have ruled the stage as one of the greatest actresses of all time, but instead she gave the world a song that has helped millions come closer to the loving heart of God when death is nigh. Because of this, Adams has touched more people than any actress of any era and given Americans a song that has been their anchor in the best and the worst of times. The *Titanic* was not unsinkable, but it appears that "Nearer, My God, to Thee" is.

ONWARD, CHRISTIAN SOLDIERS

Like many of America's favorite hymns with strong patriotic overtones, "Onward, Christian Soldiers" was actually written in England. It wasn't inspired by a war either but rather by a special day for children when peace and brotherhood were the theme for all the activities.

In 1864 Sabine Baring-Gould, an Anglican priest, was placed in charge of the children's parade for the community of Horbury Bridge, England. The annual event was one that included almost every child in the area. As was the custom, the children of Baring-Gould's village were to march to a neighboring town with banners raised high, singing songs of hope and peace. This exercise was to signify the spirit of brotherhood that binds all people together. For children who had very little in the way of toys or possessions, this was one of the most wonderful and exciting days of the year.

Baring-Gould had been sent to Horbury to minister to this community made up mainly of coal miners and their families. In truth, this was one of the bleakest parishes in all of England. The most horrific fact that echoes through this depressed area was that almost all the children lived in very poor conditions, and scores of them were not just penniless but fatherless due to mining disasters. As if to remind everyone of the sense of doom that always colored the area, a cloud of coal dust made the entire community dark and dirty. Poverty had so ensnared Horbury that church meetings were housed not in a sanctuary but in a small room above the post office. Most people, including priests who had been assigned this post in the past, thought of this town as the very end of the earth.

Obviously the church at Horbury was an assignment that most men would have deeply resented. But Baring-Gould was unique. Rather than request a quick transfer, he looked upon his parish as a wonderful opportunity to reach out and bring hope to the hopeless and faith to the faithless. In a very real sense, the pastor knew while he was there that he was ministering to those Christ called "the least of these." The priest honestly believed this made Horbury the greatest and most wonderful mission on earth.

Though Baring-Gould was a man who was available at a moment's notice to anyone in the community, the graduate of Cambridge felt a real calling to reach out to and inspire the area's children. The priest had traveled through almost all of Europe before arriving in Horbury, visiting places these children had never even imagined. In an effort to get them to apply themselves at school, Baring-Gould shared stories of the beautiful world full of opportunities that was waiting for them to explore. He assured each of them that if they worked hard and graduated from school, they could see this incredible world with their own eyes, escaping the mines to live in the bright sunshine of the lands far beyond Horbury. Needless to say, Baring-Gould endeared himself to young and old alike through his tireless work inspiring children.

As the community prepared for another Whitmonday march, Baring-Gould felt a call to do something to make the event even more special than ever. Not having the money to purchase any new banners or uniforms for the children, he decided to write a song. Unfortunately, he was unable to begin work on his piece until the night before the parade. The actual inspiration for his writing had been given to him earlier that day when he had watched children playing war in the school yard.

"It was written in a very simple fashion," Baring-Gould recalled thirty years later. "I wrote it without a thought for publication. Whitmonday is a great day for school festivals in Yorkshire, and one Whitmonday it was arranged that our school should join its forces with that of a neighboring village. I wanted the children to sing when marching from one village to the other, but I couldn't think of anything quite suitable. So I sat up at night and resolved to write something myself. 'Onward, Christian Soldiers' was the result."

The morning of the march, the priest taught the simple song to his charges. In order to make his song easy to learn, he set it to music that was familiar to almost everyone in the village—Haydn's *Symphony in D*. This classical melody was very slow and deliberate, thus providing a tool for keeping the children in step and under control as they marched down the road. As Baring-Gould would later admit, the song was really written just to use this one time. He assumed it would be forgotten as quickly as it had been composed.

"It was written in great haste," the priest acknowledged, "and I am afraid some of the rhymes are faulty. Certainly nothing has surprised me more than its popularity. I don't even remember how it got printed first, but I know that very soon it found its way into several collections."

Onward, Christian soldiers, marching as to war,
With the cross of Jesus going on before;
Christ, the royal Master, leads against the foe;
Forward into battle, see His banners go!

Chorus:
Onward, Christian soldiers, marching as to war,
With the cross of Jesus going on before.

At the sign of triumph Satan's host doth flee;
On, then, Christian soldiers, On to victory!
Hell's foundations quiver at the shout of praise;
Brothers, lift your voices, loud your anthems raise.

Chorus

Like a mighty army moves the church of God;
Brothers, we are treading where the saints have trod;
We are not divided, all one body we,
One in hope and doctrine, one in charity.

Chorus

What the saints established that I hold for true.
What the saints believèd, that I believe too.
Long as earth endureth, men the faith will hold,
Kingdoms, nations, empires, in destruction rolled.

Chorus

Crowns and thrones may perish, kingdoms rise and wane,
But the Church of Jesus constant will remain;
Gates of hell can never 'gainst that Church prevail;
We have Christ's own promise, and that cannot fail.

Chorus

Onward, then, ye people, join our happy throng,
Blend with ours your voices in the triumph song;
Glory, laud, and honor unto Christ the King;
This thro' countless ages men and angels sing.

Chorus

"Onward, Christian Soldiers" was actually printed the same year it was written, first in an English church periodical, the *Church Times*, and later in several books containing new hymns. Yet the song would not gain wide acceptance until the lyrics were matched to a different tune.

In 1871 Arthur S. Sullivan, another Englishman, was working on a new hymnal for the Church of England. When the songwriter came across a copy of Baring-Gould's children's march, he was initially impressed because he knew Baring-Gould as one of the country's best theological authors. Sullivan figured that anything Baring-Gould had penned would have great merit. As he studied "Onward, Christian Soldiers," he became mesmerized. The lyrics were radically different than anything he had ever read. The only thing that did not impress Sullivan about this new song was the music Baring-Gould had used for his score.

Unable to use it in its original form, Sullivan sat down and composed another tune to match the priest's lyrics. With great confidence, Sullivan put this arrangement in his book, *The Hymnal*. Yet even he could not have predicted the popularity and quick acceptance of this new hymn.

"Onward, Christian Soldiers" literally circled the globe within ten years of the joining of Baring-Gould's words to Sullivan's melody. It was adopted as the marching anthem of the Salvation Army, was used on foreign mission fields by thousands of missionaries, and was sung in countless Christian churches in Europe and America. Yet while the song continued to be an important facet of worship on both sides of the Atlantic, it took a world war to give this hymn a patriotic flavor.

By the middle of World War II, the leader of the Axis nations took on an almost demonic quality. As news of the treatment of POWs as well as the first rumors of the Holocaust began to filter back to the United States, no man in modern history had seemed to be so cruel and inhumane as did Hitler. Because of this image, especially for the men fighting against the Nazi war machine, this battle seemed to take on a holy stature. It was an accepted fact that millions in England and the United States felt this fight was not just for territory but for faith. So, though the German people were not demonized by the press or the free world, Hitler and his team were now seen as in league with the forces of evil. Germany and the rest of Europe had to be saved from these demonic forces. In the minds of many, it was literally good against evil for the right to control the fate of the whole world.

After a 1941 meeting between President Franklin D. Roosevelt and Prime Minister Winston Churchill on the British battleship *Prince of Wales,* Churchill requested that the Royal Navy band play "Onward, Christian Soldiers." Film taken during the occasion showed both leaders solemn in their resolve to fight until the world was again safe for all people. The next day the British head of state addressed a radio audience that included both the BBC and, later in a transcription, the United States. When he spoke he explained why the Baring-Gould hymn meant so much to him at this moment.

"We sang 'Onward, Christian Soldiers' indeed, and I felt that this was no vain presumption, but that we had the right to feel that we were serving a cause for the sake of which a trumpet has sounded from on high. When I looked upon that densely packed congregation of fighting men of the same language, of the same faith, of the same fundamental laws, of the same ideals ... it swept across me that here was the only hope, but also the sure hope, of saving the world from measureless degradation."

In the battle for Europe, Americans and Englishmen joined together often to sing "Onward, Christian Soldiers." In churches in both Britain and the United States this hymn not only united people in the fight for freedom but also served as an inspiration to battle just as hard for the right to practice faith freely as for the spoils of war.

Written for children, "Onward, Christian Soldiers" has stood the test of time as an anthem of unity and strength for all believers. Sabine Baring-Gould wanted the children of a poor village to understand that they could overcome the odds and reach their dreams. All it would take would be hard work, determination, and faith in Christ.

"Onward, Christian Soldiers" has become a song that is often used today for patriotic services because its message is really the same as the American ideal. Ideally, the United States is not a nation built on war but rather on peace, compassion, and inclusion. We have at times departed from that image, but many Americans through the years have tried to steer the nation back to this unique standpoint. The march of faith and peace, therefore, goes on under the banner of love and acceptance, and this is what "Onward, Christian Soldiers" was meant to show. Americans today would be wise to pray that this old children's song continues to inspire and guide this nation in its third century.

ROLL, JORDAN, ROLL

O n July 4, 1862, during an Independence Day parade (then called Declaration Day), thousands of blacks, just freed by Union forces, marched the streets of Washington under the Stars and Stripes. As they paraded through the nation's capital, these former slaves sang an old spiritual, "Roll, Jordan, Roll." At that time in the North very little was known about the music of black America. For those who listened to the upbeat, enthusiastic voices harmonize on the lyrics, this song appeared to be only a religious ode that spoke of life after death and the joys that could be found in heaven. Yet for the blacks, who had sung this song in the fields for years, "Roll, Jordan, Roll" carried another, but no less spiritual, meaning. In the minds of those formally bound by chains, this spiritual carried as much meaning for an Independence Day celebration as did "My Country, 'Tis of Thee" or "The Star-Spangled Banner."

By the time of the Civil War, the music sung in the fields by slaves had become a mixture of the rhythm songs of Africa's Ivory Coast and the folk tunes of the rural South. These work songs embraced a wide variety of subjects from tribal lore to romance. It was only when slave communities were taught about Jesus that the messages in their music began to center on spiritual themes. Often sung as "calls," in which a lead vocalist was answered by a chorus, these spirituals were direct and simple. Whether retelling the story of Moses or the birth of

Jesus, the Christian songs of black slaves were really Bible stories brought to life through music. As such they became an incredible tool that spread the gospel across the South to countless people of all races.

Soon, as the spirituals began to develop and the theology of the men and women who wrote them deepened, the compositions began to go beyond retelling biblical stories to express the hope found in the afterlife. In religious services, usually directed or organized by white slave owners, black men and women were told that Jesus loved them just as he did all his children. This novel concept, the very heart of Christian faith, set many blacks to questioning the validity of their being held in bondage. As they learned more about the children of Israel, as they began to grasp the fact that accepting Jesus was an act that freed people to do his will, the chains of slavery became heavier. Leading slaves to Christ no doubt contributed to many blacks seeking to gain freedom on earth as well.

In the early 1800s a wide range of spirituals, such as "Gospel Ship," described escaping slavery by leaving this world for the next. Heaven became a central theme of a large number of songs sung in the fields and at informal black worship services. For most people who had known nothing but slavery, who had no real hope of ever having any freedom, only the next world offered liberty. Thus, thoughts of heaven, the only real escape from a life in bondage, meant a great deal to the slaves in the South. Yet with the advent of the abolitionist movement and the building of the Underground Railroad, another avenue of escape opened for those in slavery. Though running away to freedom in the North

Chorus:
Roll, Jordan, roll
Roll, Jordan, roll
I want to go to Heaven when I die
To hear old Jordan roll

O brother you ought to've been there, Yes my Lord
A-sitting up in the Kingdom
To hear old Jordan roll
O sister you ought to've been there, Yes my Lord
A-sitting up in the Kingdom
To hear old Jordan roll

Chorus

O preacher you ought to've been there, Yes my Lord
A-sitting up in the Kingdom
To hear old Jordan roll
O sinner you ought to've been there, Yes my Lord
A-sitting up in the Kingdom
To hear old Jordan roll

Chorus

was extremely dangerous, the passion for living free drove many to take that chance.

A decade before the Civil War, when the Underground Railroad had become better established, news of this escape route found its way to almost every plantation in the South. Soon thousands of slaves knew where the safe houses in their area were, what they had to have and do to get to the first stop, how to travel north from one hiding place to the next, and finally, what to do to cross the Ohio River to get to the free states. As more and more of these men and women stole away in the night to ride the train to freedom, slave owners began to tighten security. Blacks were even forbidden to speak of escape or personal freedom. If they did, they were punished, usually by lashes with a whip. Yet punishment did little to stem the flow of slaves seeking freedom; it simply made the process go underground just like the railroad.

In order to keep the dream of freedom alive, slaves started hiding their quest in field music by adding another layer to the songs they sang while they worked. To the whites who were watching and listening, these spirituals seemed no different than the ones sung in the past. What slave owners didn't know was that now certain songs had dual meanings. On one level they were Christian songs of faith, but on another level they were filled with information about the Underground Railroad and other methods of escaping the South for the freedom of the North. Sadly, these songs, along with almost all other music written by slaves, all but disappeared after the Civil War.

In the 1860s and 1870s, most freed slaves did not want to sing any song that reminded them of a hopeless life spent in chains. They tried to rid themselves and their culture of all things from the shameful era of bondage. In an attempt to fit into a free world, these former slaves either wrote new songs or sang the popular odes of white America. From folk songs to hymns, blacks adopted the music of the status quo and in the process all but erased the wonderful music that was uniquely their own.

When it became obvious that many of the spirituals were being forgotten, several scholars made an effort to research the songs and save them, but because many former slaves refused to even acknowledge they had ever sung songs they now viewed as shameful, thousands were never saved. Yet thanks to the Work family of Nashville, Tennessee (pioneering black educators who transcribed and saved scores of Negro spirituals), and the Fisk College Jubilee Singers (the famous Nashville choir that performed all over the world the numbers the Works saved), the Negro spiritual was saved from complete extinction. Not only did the Fisk Singers reclaim spirituals in the last three decades of the 1800s, but their vibrant performances of these songs all across America and Europe also brought this music to mainstream white America. A great deal of the slave music that was saved found its way into hymnals where it was adopted by white Christians. Eventually, sensing the importance of the songs' message and history, even freed slaves began to reclaim their music. One of the favorites performed by the young men and women of Fisk was "Roll, Jordan, Roll."

Usually the Fisk Singers began singing this old song very slowly. Each phrase and word was emphasized and cradled as if the song were intended to be a lullaby. Yet as

159

their performance continued, the pace picked up. By the last verse, "Roll, Jordan, Roll" was running like a roaring river, racing to get to the next note, the next word, and the promise of eternal life that was just ahead. As the singers finished this song, most audiences rose to their feet to acknowledge the talent of the choir and the joy found in the old spiritual. Yet of the hundreds of thousands who heard this spiritual in the years following the Civil War, only a few former slaves understood the song's hidden message.

In "Roll, Jordan, Roll," the river that stood between this life and the next was not really the famous biblical river. When the slaves sang this song they pictured the Ohio River that separated the slave states from those that offered freedom. In the spiritual, heaven was not some place available only after death, but it was waiting in Illinois, Indiana, Ohio, and any other state where blacks had the right to live free. And death in this old song did not mean the absence of life but rather the absence of the bonds of slavery. In other words, when slaves sang "Roll, Jordan, Roll," they were singing about crossing the Ohio River to a land of freedom and putting to death a life spent in chains. It is little wonder that those who worked in the fields and sang this song often had a far-away look in their eyes.

On July 4, 1862, when the newly freed slaves marched through Washington singing "Roll, Jordan, Roll," those who listened, including President Lincoln, were awed not only by the harmonies and excitement of the tune but also by the joy they heard in the voices and the tears they witnessed streaming down the faces of these men, women, and children. Though it had been sung slowly in the fields, "Roll, Jordan, Roll" was now fast and upbeat. The sadness and the sorrow had been left behind, and those who marched in front of the capitol building on that Independence Day finally had reason to express the joy found in real freedom. "Roll, Jordan, Roll" was therefore a vocal announcement that the dream of freedom had finally arrived and that a piece of heaven could be found in this life and on this earth for men and women of every race.

STAND UP, STAND UP FOR JESUS

The decade before the Civil War was a traumatic period in the history of the United States. The issue of slavery had divided not just the North from the South but churches, communities, and even families in every corner of the country. With each passing year times grew more uncertain and attitudes more hostile. As each side stood steadfast in its convictions, to many it seemed certain the nation would be completely ripped apart. Perhaps because of the insecurity Americans felt about their own government and its ability to unite and guide its people, a great Christian revival movement crisscrossed the thirty-six states and territories. In small rural villages and sprawling cities from New York to Chicago, evangelists spoke before throngs who yearned to hear a message that contained peace, hope, and security.

The revival movement hit the nation's birthplace of liberty, Philadelphia, in 1858. Scores of preachers from all denominations packed churches with messages of salvation, rededication, and repentance. While numerous pastors drew crowds, there was one young man who seemed to garner the largest part of the public's attention.

Reverend Dudley A. Tyng was bright, well-read, and dynamic. In a city that was home to some of the greatest religious minds in the country, Tyng stood out. His bold messages demanded that people not just turn to God but serve him in every facet of their lives. Much like later evangelists such as Billy Sunday and Billy Graham, Tyng's words altered lives and lifestyles. His meetings were not just religious sessions; they were events. People would give up season-ticket seats to the theater in order to hear him. And those who listened to his messages usually responded.

On April 16, hours before one of Tyng's services was to begin, crowds started to gather outside Jaynes Hall. The building contained five thousand seats, but that was not enough. Those who arrived just before the service started were not able to get into the building to hear the charismatic Christian preacher. Yet those who did find a place would never forget what he had to say.

Tyng centered his message on Exodus 10:11: "Go now ye that are men, and serve the LORD." As he spoke on dedication and Christian commitment, the hall grew silent. Each person hung on the man's every word and movement. When he raised his voice, scores jumped from their seats. When he spoke in a whisper, heads cocked toward the pulpit. When he raised his arm, thousands craned their necks to follow the move. It was obvious to all who where there that Tyng had them in the palm of his hand, but rather than take advantage of this adulation for his own glory, the preacher used the opportunity to draw a verbal road map of how each person could meet and serve the Lord of heaven and earth.

"I must tell my Master's errand," Tyng declared that night. He then paused and held up his arm. "And I would rather that this right arm were amputated at the trunk than I should come short of my duty to you in delivering God's message."

It was one of the most remarkable revival scenes ever witnessed in the young nation's history. For the moment the rumors of war, the issues that divided North and South, and the uncertainty of tomorrow faded away. With Tyng leading the way, all eyes were on the cross. When the preacher finished his remarks and gave an altar call, more than one thousand came forward to accept Christ as their Savior.

Hours later, when the mass of people had finally departed Jaynes Hall and gone home, Dudley Tyng waved good-bye to a few close friends and headed to his own rural residence. Ironically, the man who many felt would be America's spiritual leader for the next forty years would never again preach a sermon.

A few days later, on a warm Wednesday afternoon, Tyng stood amazed as a local farm implement dealer showed the preacher a new corn sheller. As one of the preacher's mules walked in a circle harnessed to the state-of-the-art mechanical marvel, kernels literally fell off the cob. The kindly Tyng smiled and approached the hardworking mule. He softly said something to the animal, then patted him on the neck. As he did, the preacher moved too close to the machine. His sleeve caught in the gears. Tyng screamed, and the farm equipment dealer watched in horror. By the time the mule could be stopped, his right arm had been crushed and a main artery severed.

In the blink of an eye the unthinkable had happened. Though friends pulled him from the blood-drenched sheller and a doctor was summoned, nothing could be done for the dynamic Christian leader. He quickly grew weak from loss

Stand up, stand up for
    Jesus,
Ye soldiers of the cross,
Lift high His royal banner,
It must not suffer loss;
From victory unto victory
His army shall He lead,
Till every foe is vanquished
And Christ is Lord indeed.

Stand up, stand up, for
    Jesus,
The trumpet call obey;
Forth to the mighty conflict
In this His glorious day.
Ye that are men now serve
    Him
Against unnumbered foes;
Let courage rise with
    danger,
And strength to strength
    oppose.

Stand up, stand up, for
    Jesus,
Stand in His strength alone;
The arm of flesh will fail
    you —
Ye dare not trust your own;
Put on the gospel armor,
Each piece put on with
    prayer,
Where duty calls, or
    danger,
Be never wanting there.

Stand up, stand up, for
    Jesus,
The strife will not be long;
This day the noise of battle,
The next, the victor's song;
To him that overcometh
A crown of life shall be;
He with the King of glory
Shall reign eternally.

of blood, the color in his face replaced by a ghostly pale look of death. His friends rushed him to his bed, but the preacher knew there was nothing they could do. He was dying. As his loved ones gathered by his side, Tyng summoned the strength to whisper one final evangelistic charge: "Tell them to stand up for Jesus." A few moments later, as those around him sang "Rock of Ages," the preacher died.

George Duffield Jr. was horrified at the loss of his friend. A third-generation Presbyterian pastor, the son of the chaplain to the Continental Congress during the Revolutionary War, Duffield was famil-iar with suffering and death. He had preached at count-less funerals and tried to comfort hundreds of mourners. Yet to lose this mighty Christian leader just when the nation so needed his guidance seemed unfathomable. For the rest of the week the pastor tried to sort out his ideas and make some sense of the tragic loss.

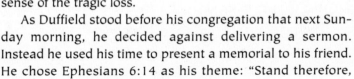

As Duffield stood before his congregation that next Sunday morning, he decided against delivering a sermon. Instead he used his time to present a memorial to his friend. He chose Ephesians 6:14 as his theme: "Stand therefore, having your loins girt about with truth, and having the breastplate of righteousness."

Many tears fell as Duffield spoke. Then after sharing with the congregation Tyng's final words, the preacher concluded the service by singing a song he had composed just for the occasion:

> *Stand up, stand up for Jesus,*
> *Ye soldiers of the cross.*
> *Lift high His royal banner,*
> *It must not suffer loss.*

Duffield sang six verses and then sat down, having no idea that what he had written would become one of the greatest hymns in the world. In truth, he believed no one would long recall what he said that April morning. His earnest prayer had been that somehow those who heard him would remember Tyng and his vibrant witness.

When it was first presented, "Stand Up, Stand Up for Jesus" had been coupled to a popular British tune written by George J. Webb. Duffield had probably chosen the tune simply because it fit his poem's meter. Yet within a year, Webb's "'Tis Dawn, the Lark Is Singing" had been forgotten and the melody had become forever associated with the new hymn. It was also spreading across the country like a fever.

"Stand Up, Stand Up for Jesus" was used as a marching song during the Civil War. Union troops sang it as early as 1862. Within two years it was common to hear Confederates marching to the words as well. Several soldiers' letters to home mentioned that at night troops on both sides of the lines would sing the song in unison. As strange as this seemed, it would often be in the context of war in which this hymn of peace, love, and conviction would have its greatest impact.

Within fifty years of Tyng's death, his final words were being sung in hundreds of languages and dialects. After World War II, U.S. soldiers heard it sung by children during the occupation of Japan. American military men and women heard children sing the Christian standard again in Korea and Vietnam. It seems this hymn has greeted American service personnel everywhere they have gone. "Stand Up, Stand Up for Jesus" was probably the first American hymn to gain acclaim around the world.

In a Pacific battlefield hospital during World War II, another time of great American uncertainty and insecurity, wounded soldiers rested under a canvas tent. As the men waited to be shipped out, a medic rigged a radio to pick up the Armed Forces Network. In the tropical heat, badly injured men had their first chance in weeks to hear the sounds of home. At one point just before dusk, the station made a dramatic change of pace and played a familiar religious standard.

As the music filled the air, the men in the tent grew silent. As a choir sang "Stand Up, Stand Up for Jesus," a gravely injured young man pulled himself to a sitting position on his cot. He then grabbed the tent's support pole and willed himself to stand. As doctors, nurses, and other patients looked on, the weakened man held himself erect and at attention until the song had finished. He then collapsed. A day before he had stood up for his country in the face of ferocious enemy fire. Now, as a Christian soldier, he had stood up for his Savior. It was a powerful witness that touched the battle-hardened men in a way no sermon ever had.

"Stand Up, Stand Up for Jesus" is perhaps the greatest revival song of all time. It does not ask, rather it demands that men and women everywhere fully display their beliefs and their faith to all those around them. Christian believers everywhere—in churches, on battlefields, and at home—have responded to Dudley Tyng's charge in a way that has made this more than just a hymn but an American classic of faith, love, and duty. It may have been inspired by a dying man's words and first presented by a preacher who thought no one would remember his memorial message, but "Stand Up, Stand Up for Jesus" has become a song to live by. Though Dudley Tyng has been forgotten, what he stood for still rallies Christian Americans to the cross.

THE STAR-SPANGLED BANNER

"The Star-Spangled Banner" is the national anthem of the United States of America due to one town's love and commitment to one of its own citizens and another man's quest for justice. Without a community's concern driving them to action, the events that inspired this famous song would have never taken place and Francis Scott Key would never have seen the flag that waved over Fort McHenry in 1814.

Dr. William Beanes was the beloved physician of Upper Marlboro, Maryland, for several years before war broke out between the United States and England. A loyal patriot, he was so respected by those in power that he was entrusted with the most important papers of the state government. His job was to make sure these papers did not fall into enemy hands. In accepting this awesome and important duty, the doctor had pledged to guard the documents with his life. Then Beanes, in an act that was viewed as both stupid and shrewd, chose to hide most of the government materials in the city jail. During the first two years of the war literally thousands of English troops, on their way to and from action, passed through the building without ever noting the significant boxes stacked against a cell wall.

Beanes did not let his loyal American stance and his work for his government stand in the way of what he felt was his Christian duty as a doctor. He used his expertise and talents to treat whomever needed help. Hundreds of injured British troops

170

had their wounds tended to by the kindly old man. Scores owed their lives to his skills.

In late August 1814 the doctor encountered two drunken British regulars who had deserted their unit. The staggering soldiers were creating havoc throughout Upper Marlboro. The Brits were so inebriated that they would not listen to reason and insisted on rejoining their unit. Finally, when Beanes had taken as much as he could of their surly attitudes, he disarmed the men, marched them to the jail, and locked them up. A few hours later one of the prisoners managed to escape. When the now sober Redcoat told his story to his regiment's commander, the British marched back into town in force. They sought out the doctor, arrested him, and took him to the jail. Beanes's heart must have been pounding like a bass drum as he watched uniformed Englishmen brush against some of the state's most important documents. Yet in spite of the fact that they were literally surrounding them, the British failed to notice the boxes of papers. In one of the colossal oversights of the war, they simply released the other British prisoner, tossed Beanes onto a wagon, and took him with them back to Baltimore.

Most towns would have been grateful to have escaped this enemy invasion with the capture of only one man. Yet Upper Marlboro was different. They were as loyal to Dr. Beanes as he was to his nation's cause. Rather than simply allow the doctor to spend the remainder of the war in chains, a committee of town leaders decided to take action. After an informal meeting, they traveled to Georgetown to seek legal advice from Francis Scott Key.

Key was a well-known patriot, an army veteran, and one of the best legal minds in the New World. He listened to the

Oh, say, can you see, by the dawn's early light,
What so proudly we hailed at the twilight's last gleaming?
Whose broad stripes and bright stars, thro' the perilous fight,
O'er the ramparts we watched, were so gallantly streaming?
And the rockets' red glare, the bombs bursting in air,
Gave proof thro' the night that our flag was still there.
Oh, say, does that star-spangled banner yet wave
O'er the land of the free, and the home of the brave?

On the shore, dimly seen thro' the mists of the deep,
Where the foe's haughty host in dread silence reposes,
What is that which the breeze, o'er the towering steep,
As it fitfully blows, half conceals, half discloses?
Now it catches the gleam of the morning's first beam,
In full glory reflected, now shines on the stream:
'Tis the star-spangled banner; oh, long may it wave
O'er the land of the free, and the home of the brave.

And where is that band, who so vauntingly swore
That the havoc of war and the battle's confusion,
A home and a country should leave us no more?
Their blood has washed out their foul footsteps' pollution;
No refuge could save the hireling and slave
From the terror of flight or the gloom of the grave.
And the star-spangled banner in triumph doth wave
O'er the land of the free, and the home of the brave.

O, thus be it ever when freemen shall stand
Between their loved homes and the war's desolation;
Blest with vict'ry and peace, may the Heav'n-rescued land
Praise the Pow'r that hath made and preserved us as a nation!
Then conquer we must, when our cause it is just;
And this be our motto: "In God is our trust!"
And the star-spangled banner in triumph shall wave
O'er the land of the free, and the home of the brave.

Upper Marlboro delegation, reviewed the circumstances of Beanes's arrest, and agreed to take the case. As the British soldiers had been drunk and disorderly and had breached the peace before being detained, Key felt sure British law would support the doctor's action. Yet to gain an audience with Redcoat officials, he knew he would need help.

The lawyer contacted Col. John Skinner, an American agent for prisoner exchange, and, on September 3 the two of them set sail for Baltimore on a tiny sloop. The English were preparing to attack Fort McHenry and lay siege to Baltimore, so it took four long days for the men to gain an audience with Admiral Alexander Cochrane. On the British ship *Tonnant*, Key laid out the evidence and presented his argument for freeing the American physician. Cochrane listened to Key and reviewed the facts, but he refused to release Beanes in spite of the fact that English law obviously had been broken with the doctor's arrest. Just as the Americans were about to be dismissed, Key, who like the fictional Perry Mason was always prepared with a rebuttal, pulled a stack of papers from his coat pocket. As the admiral listened, Key began to read letters from British troops who owed their lives to the skills and compassion of the American doctor. These testimonials, taken from the doctor's own desk drawer, caused Cochrane to reverse his decision.

Key had won freedom for Beanes. Yet as the lawyer soon discovered, that freedom came with a catch. Key, Skinner, and Beanes were ordered to remain on the British ship until the battle of Fort McHenry was concluded. In other words, the trio was forced to remain in custody until September 16.

The bombardment of Baltimore and Fort McHenry began just after dawn on September 13, 1814. For twenty-five hours the British fleet sustained a relentless attack by lobbing fifteen hundred bombshells weighing over two hundred pounds each at the American fort. It was a spectacular show, but it was not very effective. As Key, Beanes, and Skinner observed, many of the bombs blew up in the air long before they struck their intended targets. English-made congreve rockets also lit up the sky but failed to come close to their targets. The British Navy was unleashing an awesome show, one that looked like it was creating great damage, but in truth it was little more than a fireworks display.

From their positions, Key and the other two Americans probably thought the American forces were literally being blown to bits. It certainly appeared that way from their vantage point eight miles away. Still, the mere fact that the British had continued to bomb Fort McHenry all night long proved that the American forces had not given up the fight. Finally, just before dawn on the fourteenth, the British quit firing and all was quiet. Key fully expected to see McHenry in ruins. Yet as he picked up his telescope, his spyglass was filled with the image of a huge red, white, and blue flag flying above the harbor. His heart leaped as he realized the Americans had held their ground and the English had given up. After two years of constant defeat and retreat, the United States could claim a decisive battle. The tide of the war turned.

Just as Dr. Beanes had brought Key to the harbor, General George Armistead had made it possible for the attorney to spy McHenry's flag. The fort's commander had hired Mary Young Pickersgill, a seamstress, to sew a banner so large that it could be seen for miles away. The banner took more than four hundred yards of bunting. The stars were twenty-six inches across, and the stripes were two feet wide. Set atop the fort's almost one-hundred-foot flagpole, the forty-two-feet-wide and thirty-feet-high flag could be seen from ten miles away. Because of its size, on that September morning Key could easily see that the Americans had taken the best the British had to offer and their banner had not even dipped, much less fallen.

Seeing that sight, feeling the blood rushing to his heart and his spirit soaring to new heights, the attorney pulled a letter from his pocket, perhaps even one of those that had won Beanes his freedom. On that scrap of paper, Key began to jot down the words to a poem that would come to define this moment in American history. The lawyer finally finished the four verses of the "Defense of Fort McHenry" two days later while staying at Baltimore's Indian Queen Hotel.

One of the first men to read Key's poem was his brother-in-law, Judge J. H. Nicholson. Nicholson felt that all loyal Americans should read the work and had it printed and distributed throughout the area. It created such a stir that the *Baltimore Patriot* published the poem on September 20. Within weeks almost every paper in the United States had printed Key's poetry. Yet for the moment, it was strictly a poem, not a song.

Key's "Defense of Fort McHenry" happened to fit perfectly the meter of an English melody, "An Anacreon in Heaven." As the lawyer had used the English drinking song two years earlier when writing a musical tribute to Commodore Stephen Decatur, he might have had the tune in mind when he wrote his poem. While exactly when Key coupled the verses to the melody will forever be debated, it is most likely that John Stafford Smith, the loyal Englishman who wrote the tune in London around 1780, did not approve of the marriage of American lyrics and his melody. Nevertheless, in October 1814 Baltimore actor Ferdinand Durang first sang "Defense of Fort McHenry" at Captain McCauley's tavern, and the union of the words and music were linked forever afterward.

For more than a century "The Star-Spangled Banner" was used by the United States Army and Navy as the national anthem. Yet until the Hoover administration, the nation did not officially recognize Key's work as being anything more than just another patriotic song. Finally in 1931, by an act of Congress, the song that described one of the nation's most inspiring military moments was made the official anthem of the United States.

It was an act of compassion that brought the men of Upper Marlboro to Francis Scott Key's door. It was an act of courage that caused the attorney to take a noble doctor's case and sail into the midst of the world's greatest navy. While the law did not help the lawyer win his case and free Dr. Beanes, the Christian charity the physician extended to wounded enemies of his country during a time of brutal war ultimately secured his release. Then, only because the Americans were forced to wait for the outcome of a spectacular battle, they were given an opportunity to witness one of the greatest moments in their nation's young history.

Some would say that fate placed Francis Scott Key in Baltimore Harbor at the very moment he found the inspiration to gift America with what would become its national anthem. Yet to those of faith, it could only have been God's hand, set in motion by love, compassion, courage, and the convictions of believers such as Dr. Beanes and his friends, that brought the lawyer to the moment when he witnessed and recorded the thrilling sight of the star-spangled banner waving triumphantly over Fort McHenry.

THE STATUE OF LIBERTY

*I*n 1974 a gospel music singer stood at the rail of a cruise ship as it made its way through New York Harbor. The sun had already set, and the city lights sparkled all around where the young man stood. Tired from hours of performing, he barely noted the beauty that was before him until he heard excited voices saying, "Look at that!" "Wow!" "Incredible!"

Glancing up, Neil Enloe suddenly found himself almost face-to-face with the greatest symbol of liberty that man had ever constructed. This towering image of freedom left him speechless. With his heart racing and pride welling up in his soul, the Wood River, Illinois, native must have been moved in much the same way that French artist Frederic-Auguste Bartholdi was when he initially viewed Lady Liberty in New York. Though these two creative spirits were from different centuries, a vision of American freedom would forever unite them in inspiration. What each man constructed from his personal vision ultimately touched millions and paved the road to liberty and joy—and in the case of Enloe's gift, eternal life.

In 1865 Frenchman Edouard Rene Lefebvre de Laboulaye, scholar, jurist, and abolitionist, held a dinner. The respected educator and politician wanted to form a group of national leaders dedicated to creating a republican government modeled on America's Constitution. During the evening, Laboulaye pointed out to his colleagues that there was "a genuine flow of sympathy" between France and America. He even called the nations "the two sisters." He went ahead to note that America's centennial was little more than a decade away. Then he paused, as if an idea had suddenly come to him, before adding, "Wouldn't it be wonderful if the people of France gave the United States a great monument as a lasting memorial to independence and thereby showed that the French government was also dedicated to the idea of human liberty?"

Attending the dinner that night was a friend and sculptor named Frederic-Auguste Bartholdi. The concept of giving the United States a birthday present fascinated Bartholdi. Even days after the meeting he could not let go of the notion. Ultimately he decided he would be the one to create such a gift.

In 1871, armed with a vague idea of what he wanted to do, Bartholdi sailed for America. He could not wait to visit the United States for the first time; he'd read so much about the vast frontier that he considered the new land to be an almost magical place. Yet even he could not have predicted the emotions that flooded his soul when American shores finally came into view. Bartholdi was overwhelmed, and his eyes filled with tears when his ship made its way into New York Harbor. He later wrote, "The picture that is presented to the view when one arrives in New York is marvelous, when, after some days of voyaging, in the pearly radiance of a beautiful morning is revealed the magnificent spectacle of those immense cities (Brooklyn and Manhattan), of those rivers extending as far as the eye can reach, festooned with masts and flags; when one awakes, so to speak, in the midst of that interior sea covered with vessels . . . it is thrilling. It

In New York Harbor stands a lady
With a torch raised to the sky.
And all who see her know she stands for
Liberty for you and I.

I'm so proud to be called an American;
To be named with the brave and the free.
I will honor our flag and our trust in God,
And the Statue of Liberty.

On lonely Golgotha stood a cross
With my Lord raised to the sky.
And all who kneel there live forever,
As all the saved can testify.

I'm so glad to be called a Christian;
To be named with the ransomed and whole.
As the statue liberates the citizen,
So the cross liberates the soul.

Coda:
Oh the cross is my Statue of Liberty;
It was there that my soul was set free.
Unashamed I'll proclaim that a rugged cross
Is my Statue of Liberty.

is indeed the New World, which appears in its majestic expanse with the ardor of its glowing life."

Bartholdi quickly became even more convinced that it was his calling to give this free land a monument to the liberty that each citizen held so dear. He spent his spare hours sketching his vision of what that gift should be. With his first view of America in mind, Bartholdi went on numerous sight-seeing trips to a host of different locations throughout the eastern half of the United States. During the course of his tours, the sculptor, who brought with him letters of introduction from artists and government officials in France, met President Ulysses S. Grant, Henry Wadsworth Longfellow, and Horace Greeley. He told each of them of his plans for a huge statue that represented liberty. He also shared with the men that he felt New York Harbor would be the perfect place for such a memorial.

The artist then produced a sketch of his plans for a monument he called "Liberty Enlightening the World." He was such an incredible salesman that it seemed every influential American he met encouraged the Frenchman to continue his work and assured him the United States would welcome such a gift. Yet it was four long years before enough private donations could be raised in France to support the construction of Bartholdi's vision of liberty. The time spent waiting to put form to his inspiration all but killed the impatient sculptor.

Alexandre-Gustave Eiffel, who later built the Eiffel Tower, was commissioned to construct the statue's frame. Bartholdi oversaw the rest of the work. Yet things did not go smoothly, and Liberty did not come together quickly. She missed her date with the centennial. She also missed several more potential dedication dates. But on June 15, 1885,

Bartholdi's vision finally arrived in New York, packaged in several hundred packing crates. Over a year later the pieces finally became one, and the beautiful woman stood proudly as the tallest structure in the teeming American metropolis.

On October 28, 1886, more than one million people lined New York's streets to watch the Liberty parade. Another twenty thousand people marched in this moving carnival of patriotic pride. To give the event an even more festive attitude, office boys tossed spools of tape from the top of tall buildings, thus beginning the tradition of the New York ticker tape parade. As a throng looked out over the sun-drenched harbor, speeches were made and bands played American music. Finally, after hours of preliminaries, Bartholdi pulled the cord on the huge cloth that draped the statue, and Lady Liberty's gleaming copper face was unveiled to the world. After studying the noble gift for some time, President Grover Cleveland promised, "We will not forget that Liberty has made here her home, nor shall her chosen altar be neglected."

From that day forward, Lady Liberty stood greeting all who came to visit or emigrate to the United States. To Americans as well as those who hoped to someday become citizens, this great statue represented freedom. Even ninety years after its construction, when scores of other city buildings towered over her, the Statue of Liberty remained such an awe-inspiring sight that teenagers sailing by on a cruise ship were taken aback. One of those on board with the kids that night was Neil Enloe.

In 1974 Enloe was singing with the Couriers, a gospel music group from Pennsylvania. They had been hired by the National Assemblies of God to perform for twenty-four hundred youth from churches in New York and New Jersey. The venue for the night was a five-decked vessel that was used for sight-seeing trips. The ship was huge, but it had been built with a main ballroom that seated only four hundred. As the Couriers had been hired to sing to all of the kids who had made the trip, they had to do six different shows. This meant the singers received only ten-minute breaks between sets. It was during one of their final breaks that Enloe decided to stroll the decks and get some fresh air. He walked out just in time to see the fully lighted Statue of Liberty towering over the dark waters of New York Harbor. It was a moment that would change his life forever.

"I had never seen the statue that close," Enloe recalled. "It seemed to be so near I could almost touch it. Suddenly everything that was American welled up in me. Maybe it was because of my Midwest roots and the fact that I had not seen it on a regular basis, but seeing the statue like this made me so proud to be an American."

For the next few minutes Enloe stood transfixed, unable to take his eyes off Lady Liberty. Overwhelmed, he finally turned to one of the other members of his group and said, "This thing represents our liberty, but I have another citizenship that also represents my liberty." For the singer, that second citizenship was in God's family.

"There had to be a song in what I had just seen and felt," Enloe told a friend later that night. He vowed to put his observations and feelings on paper. Yet just like Bartholdi had been forced to toil for years to complete the work on Lady Liberty, the American singer would spend months trying to turn his inspiration into a musical message.

"I really believe songs that make sense have to be carefully crafted," Enloe explained. In this case, with a song inspired by a moment that meant so much to him, he was not going to rush his work. Three months after the cruise, after he had written and rewritten the song numerous times, he finally had something he was willing to share with the other members of his group.

"I knew I had something of a greater magnitude than anything I had done before," the writer recalled. But even Enloe didn't know if anyone else would get worked up by his personal convictions set to music. The immediately positive reaction of gospel music fans indicated that the songwriter and the public were of like mind. "The Statue of Liberty" quickly became one of the most popular Christian songs of the era. After it pulled down gospel music's highest award, a Dove, and topped the Christian music charts for weeks, a host of friends congratulated Enloe on tapping into the spirit of the bicentennial. Though none of them doubted the sincere message of the song, most considered "The Statue of Liberty" a clever marketing tool meant to cash in on America's patriotic fever.

"I wish I had been that bright," Enloe laughed, "but in truth it was something I didn't even think about." The man had simply been inspired by a moment when he saw Lady Liberty in a new light. He then came to fully realize the importance of the faith that the light of Christ had already placed in his soul.

"The Statue of Liberty" became such a dynamic American gospel favorite that it is still being requested and recorded today. The song boldly combines patriotism and faith while clearly spelling out the importance of each. A great gift that a French sculptor gave to the United States inspired an American songwriter to compose a personal testimony that explained that the greatest gift available to everyone in America is actually the everlasting freedom of salvation. That makes "The Statue of Liberty" not only one of the most uniquely American gospel songs ever written but one of the best too!

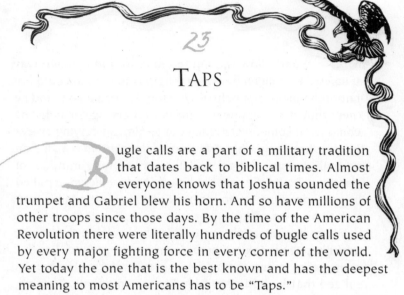

TAPS

Bugle calls are a part of a military tradition that dates back to biblical times. Almost everyone knows that Joshua sounded the trumpet and Gabriel blew his horn. And so have millions of other troops since those days. By the time of the American Revolution there were literally hundreds of bugle calls used by every major fighting force in every corner of the world. Yet today the one that is the best known and has the deepest meaning to most Americans has to be "Taps."

The most commonly repeated story of the origin of "Taps" is probably more legend than fact. In truth it was a Civil War general who decided to Americanize the evening or last call bugle tune that gave birth to what everyone now recognizes as "Taps." But there is a beauty and grace in the unproved legend of the song's origin that has come to define not just the spiritual qualities of the tune but the heart, compassion, and love of America, as well as the real tragedy of the Civil War.

In 1862 a Union officer named Robert Ellicombe was involved in heavy fighting near Harrison's Landing, Virginia. In the midst of the battle the captain heard the haunting cries of an injured soldier. A fog had rolled in, and visibility was only a few feet. Unable to see the wounded man, Ellicombe was forced to rely on his ears. As there was no static battlefront that day, the officer knew his search might well take him into enemy territory. The wise thing would have been to return to his men and allow the injured man to find his own way to safety. Yet Ellicombe was a religious man who could not ignore the pleas of a helpless person. He had a son, and he knew that if his boy was injured and crying for help, he would want someone to reach out to him. So defying everything he had taught his own troops, the captain crawled on his belly toward the cries. After several long minutes of searching, he finally saw the bloody body. Ellicombe pulled the wounded man up on his back and slowly made his way back to his own camp.

When he was safely surrounded by his men, the officer carefully put the injured man down on the ground. For the first time he noted the soldier's gray uniform. He grimly realized that he had risked his life for an enemy. Turning away, he cried out for a medic. Ellicombe then knelt down beside the Rebel, intent on assuring the man that help was on its way. As the officer began to speak, the Confederate trooper turned his head and looked up. It was at that moment that Ellicombe realized the young man was his own son. Soon after their eyes met, the boy died.

For several hours Ellicombe grieved while fighting went on all around him. Finally, when the battle ended for the day, he went to his superior officer and asked to bury his son with full military honors, including a rifle salute. Ellicombe's request was quickly denied. Even though the boy had been his son, the captain was told, he was still the enemy. Sadly the father returned to the place where his son's body rested.

This part of the old story is probably completely true. Thousands of men from the same families fought against each other during this bloody struggle. Many fathers found

the bodies of their sons on battlefields during the
Civil War. Yet what cannot be proven is what happened at
the younger Ellicombe's burial. Legend has it that the father
found a piece of paper in the boy's pocket that contained
the music for a bugle call entitled "Taps." As the importance
of this song to his son seemed evident by the young man's
desire to keep it with him at all times, the father ordered his
own bugler to play "Taps" over his son's freshly dug grave.

Could the final chapter of this story be true? Yes, the
"Taps" created by a Union general might well have found its
way into a Confederate soldier's pocket and, as the song was
newly composed, the Union forces under the command of
Ellicombe might well have not heard it yet. But this was
surely not the first time "Taps" was used at a military funeral.

At the beginning of the Civil War many Union buglers
played a melody from Silas Casey's book *Tactics* to signal
that it was time for bed. Yet this song was not required as
a last call. Some commanding officers had their own
favorite numbers they substituted for the call in *Tactics*. In
midsummer 1862 General Daniel Butterfield found that
everywhere he traveled there were different songs being
played at the end of the day. He was also told that the one
used most often had actually been written by a Frenchman. The Union officer decided that if he was fighting to
keep America united as one people under one government,
then he was going to use only American music to signal
his own army. There would be no French, English, or
German songs used while he was in command. So the
leader of Meroll's Division, Fitz-John Porter's Corp, Army
of the Potomac, decided to create his own musical version

of "Taps." When he finished his simple melody, he sent for his bugler. The bugler later wrote a letter that included his memories of that day and the manner in which the Butterfield song spread across the Civil War battlefields and into military tradition.

One day, soon after the seven days battles on the Peninsular, when the Army of the Potomac was lying in camp at Harrison's Landing, General Daniel Butterfield, then commanding our Brigade, sent for me, and showing me some notes on a staff written in pencil on the back of an envelope, asked me to sound them on my bugle. I did this several times, playing the music as written. He changed it somewhat, lengthening some notes and shortening others, but retaining the melody as he first gave it to me. After getting it to his satisfaction, he directed me to sound that call for Taps thereafter in place of the regulation call.

The music was beautiful on that still summer night, and was heard far beyond the limits of our Brigade. The next day I was visited by several buglers from neighboring Brigades, asking for copies of the music, which I gladly furnished.

I think no general order was issued from army headquarters authorizing the substitution of this for the regulation call, but as each brigade commander exercised his own discretion in such minor matters, the call was gradually taken up through the Army of the Potomac.

The song Butterfield supposedly wrote sounded a great deal like an existing bugle call, "Scott's Tattoo." "Tattoo" had long been used to inform men at military bases that it was time to put their lanterns out and go to bed. Yet even if he only arranged "Taps" and did not write the song, Butterfield was the person who lifted the tune from obscurity and positioned it to become one of the two best-known bugle calls in the world. While it had taken almost one hundred years for "Taps" to become the only song used for last call by the U.S. Army, it took only a few months more for the song to become a way of honoring a fallen soldier.

During this time only a handful of soldiers owned a watch, so the tunes a bugler played and the position of the sun were the most commonly used methods of telling time. As the battle lines of the North and South were also very close together and as fighting usually ended at dusk, there can be little doubt those wearing gray quickly understood what this new Union bugle call meant. In truth, many Confederates who heard the call retired to their bedrolls at the same time. Yet it was also the close proximity of lines during the Civil War that led to using "Taps" for something much more grave than a good-night signal.

Just months after "Taps" had been adopted by much of the Union army, a northern cannoneer was killed. A grave was hurriedly dug near the place were the man fell. At the time military protocol, which was almost always followed to the letter, demanded that the dead trooper be honored with a traditional three-volley salute from members of a rifle brigade. On that day the fighting had been fierce. The men in blue were hiding in a wooded area with Confederate soldiers all around them. Captain John C. Tidball of Battery A, 2nd Artillery, knew that a rifle salute would probably mean sure death to every man in his squad. Though it went against military regulations, he would not risk his men's life just to honor a man who had already died. Yet as he watched the grave being filled, he wondered what he could do to fully honor the departed man's sacrifice. As this soldier had given his life for his country, a simple prayer just did not seem enough. The inspiration hit. Because death was a last call for life, Tidball ordered his bugler to quietly play "Taps." As the men listened to the song, they all agreed the musical tribute was much more meaningful and befitting a graveside farewell than was a volley of gunfire. This was the first time "Taps" was used as a way to mark the end of a life.

But what of the legend of Captain Ellicombe and his son? Did the father really find the music for this bugle call in his son's pocket, and did he order it played for much different reasons than had Captain Tidball? It is very possible. During the Civil War both sides shared their music with each other. All of the popular patriotic songs of the era, including "Rally Round the Flag" and "Battle Hymn of the Republic," had both Southern and Northern lyrics. The haunting beauty of "Taps" might well have been noticed and picked up by Confederate forces who overheard it played across enemy lines. With this in mind, Ellicombe's son could have even transposed "Taps" for himself or another bugler. Thus the legend might well have been true, and this story might mark the second time "Taps" was employed in what would become its most important roll, a final salute to a fallen hero.

Validating this story would also bring together the greatest irony of the Civil War. Millions of Americans were separated over political issues, fighting to the death on land that both called home. Twenty-eight notes blown on a single mournful instrument united soldiers from the North and the South not in victory or life but in tragic death. "Taps" was never meant to be used as a final farewell for a fallen soldier, nor was the old bugle call ever supposed to take on the reverence of a hymn. Yet the spiritual quality of "Taps" has emerged because of the hope and faith of those who have heard the song played at graveside funeral services. Like a lonely wolf howling in the night, "Taps" has become one of the saddest strains ever to be conceived by man. Yet this old military salute has also evolved into a spiritual anthem, a musical bridge between earth and heaven for countless American men and women. Thus, as a tune that salutes the unselfish service of men and women whose devotion to duty and country set them apart from their peers, this song now signifies life built on faith, hope, and love. So "Taps" no longer signifies just the end of a mortal life but also the beginning of one that will never end.

WE SHALL OVERCOME

One of the most wonderful elements of the story of the Civil Rights movement in the fifties and sixties concerns the music that drove so many of the rallies and demonstrations. The most popular anthem for black American rights was actually adapted from a song written by a man who began life as a slave and rose to become one of the most influential and respected men in the city of Philadelphia. Charles Tindley therefore represented the potential and power of African-Americans decades before the United States finally gave blacks equal access to the freedoms first ordered by President Abraham Lincoln and guaranteed by the Constitution.

Charles Tindley was born a slave in Maryland in 1851. His mother died when he was an infant, and his father was sold on the auction block before the boy even learned how to walk. He was raised on a plantation by servants until the end of the Civil War when he, like millions of other blacks, was finally set free. Yet at the age of fourteen the boy already understood that freedom was little more than rhetoric. Even if you were no longer considered someone else's property, poverty and oppression still trapped you in a world with no promise and little hope.

As a teen Tindley did the same field chores for the same people who had once owned him. Fourteen hours a day, six days a week he toiled for little more than room and board. Yet at night, while other sharecroppers rested, Tindley ran barefoot more than ten miles to a night school that had been opened for former slaves. The young man sensed that education might allow him to overcome some of the hurdles that met blacks at every turn. Therefore, giving up sleep, he spent hours each night doing extra studying.

Tindley first put his education to use in church. He was the only person who worshiped in the tiny clapboard building who could actually read the Bible. Yet just reading the Bible was not enough. Once he mastered English, he began to learn Greek and Hebrew, math and science. Years of labor in the fields, studying, and hearing God's Word on Sunday filled the now six-foot-four-inch young man with a desire to do more than just plow someone else's ground. He believed the Lord had something greater planned for his life. Even though other blacks told him he would never be able to rise above being a poor farmhand, Tindley refused to quit studying or dreaming. He honestly believed that with faith he could overcome any obstacle he encountered.

After marrying Daisy Henry, Tindley moved to Philadelphia and secured a position as the janitor at the John Wesley Methodist Episcopal Church. Progressive, evangelical, a meeting place for Philadelphia's black community, this was one of the largest African-American churches in the nation. As the former slave worked and worshiped in the same building, Tindley was exposed to some of the greatest speakers and thinkers of the time. Within a year of his move to the north, Tindley felt sure he knew what the Lord had planned for him—he was meant to be a preacher. The impressive man quickly found a church that needed a minister, thus giving himself completely to his call.

Tindley had grown up singing in the fields. What had started as a way to pass the time had now grown into a passion. Realizing that music meant as much to the rest of the black community as it did to him, Tindley began to introduce original songs with his Sunday morning messages. Some of the preacher's compositions, like "Stand By Me" and "When the Morning Comes," did more than inspire those in his congregation, they made their way into the city's white community as well. Soon Tindley's songs were being sung in white churches all across the United States. Using music as the door, the preacher began to walk the streets of the city, reaching out to the lost and poor of every race.

Tindley's real power was not fully realized, however, until he was called to pastor Philadelphia's East Calvary Methodist Church. His preaching and dynamic leadership quickly built the average attendance from a few hundred to thousands. A building program expanded the sanctuary seating to five thousand, but within a year the huge auditorium was still able to hold only half the church's active members. Yet the growth, as well as the messages heard inside the church, were just a small part of Tindley's ministry.

At a time when most black Americans tried to keep a low profile, Tindley stood tall. He united the African-American community in Philadelphia with his strong ministry. Taking his work beyond the walls of his church, he began missions that helped poor people save money, find jobs, get home loans, and obtain education. He organized food and clothing drives, found shelter for homeless people, and built a soup kitchen in his church's basement. Walking through the community every day, he sought out beggars and gave them both food and spiritual guidance. He walked into bars and

We shall overcome,
We shall overcome,
We shall overcome some day,
Oh, deep in my heart,
I do believe
We shall overcome some day

We'll walk hand in hand,
We'll walk hand in hand,
We'll walk hand in hand some
    day,
Oh, deep in my heart
I do believe
We shall overcome some day.

We shall all be free,
We shall all be free,
We shall all be free some day,
Oh, deep in my heart
I do believe
We shall overcome some day.

We are not afraid,
We are not afraid,
We are not afraid some day,

Oh, deep in my heart
I do believe
We shall overcome some day.

We are not alone,
We are not alone,
We are not alone some day,
Oh, deep in my heart
I do believe
We shall overcome some day.

The whole wide world around,
The whole wide world around,
The whole wide world around
    some day,
Oh, deep in my heart
I do believe
We shall overcome some day.

We shall overcome,
We shall overcome,
We shall overcome some day,
Oh, deep in my heart
I do believe
We shall overcome some day.

bordellos and shared the gospel without judging. He knocked on the doors of homes, businesses, and schools, encouraging everyone he met to take the high road, to give as they had received.

Maybe it was because of his peaceful activism as well as his quiet pride that the people who came in contact with Tindley sensed that this former slave was very different from other men, white or black. He was able to overcome every stereotype and barrier, transcending race at a time when few dared to try. By 1910 over half of those who gathered to listen to Tindley preach on Sunday were white. Prominent white seminaries of the day even sent their students to hear his sermons.

Tindley had overcome much to rise to power. He had known the bonds of slavery, oppression, and poverty, yet he had not been held down. Still, he was acutely aware that the hard life facing most blacks at this time gave them little hope, comfort, or joy. Many of the people in his congregation felt trapped. They knew they would never have riches or even equal rights. Not as strong or bold as Tindley, most

African-Americans of this era had grown to accept the fact that they were viewed as second-class citizens, and because of this their spirits were broken.

The concept of overcoming any barrier with God's help became one that Tindley constantly preached. He also never ceased emphasizing that God would help blacks rise out of their circumstances if they had faith and would come together as a people. In his most famous sermon he hit on this very point. "You've never seen a peach tree eat its own peaches," he said, "but you have seen a tree so laden with fruit that its branches reached the ground so a toddler can pick and partake. Our lives should be like that tree. Not what we maintain for ourselves, but what we give to others, as God gave His Son. I want to be like that tree, serve others, share what I can with others."

In Tindley's mind power was not in one individual but in men and women bonded together to do the Lord's work. This work included lifting the blacks to a place where their race was seen as equal to whites.

One Sunday morning Tindley looked out at a congregation that was beaten down and discouraged. Unlike their preacher, they did not have the courage to move forward. In an effort to motivate each of them to believe in themselves, he sang an autobiographical song, "I'll Overcome Some Day." Part old spiritual and part new ideas, this moving Christian ballad might have inspired a few blacks of the day to strive to be recognized for their talents and potential, but none went on to begin a movement that would change the African-American's place in society.

Tindley had been dead for almost three decades when Dr. Martin Luther King Jr., Rosa Parks, and others finally responded to the charge the preacher had given to his congregation on countless occasions. In the late 1950s the message finally caught on, and blacks joined together to form a movement designed to overcome a century of discrimination. "I'll Overcome Some Day" became "We Shall Overcome" and was turned into an anthem for the Civil Rights movement. Led by Tindley's spirit, the movement he tried to begin through example and motivational words finally succeeded. It did not happen quickly; it took a great deal of suffering and anguish. But a full one hundred years after they gained their freedom, African-Americans finally gained a voice through legislation, voters' rights, court decisions, and general recognition.

Charles Tindley was born a slave, but he died a free man. It wasn't just Lincoln who freed him, it was also Jesus Christ. Noting the great man's passing in July of 1933, the *Negro Digest* labeled him "Lincoln in Ebony." The church where he preached is now named after him and still welcomes worshipers to the building on the corner of Broad and Fitzwater. A street he once walked reaching out to the poor is now named for him too. Yet his greatest legacy might well be composing what would become the musical charge for the Civil Rights movement. Long after he gave the example of how to overcome, millions finally dared to follow his lead. Like Tindley, they didn't just sing "I'll Overcome Some Day," they lived it. Therefore, because of the dream it helped fulfill, the spiritual "We Shall Overcome" is one of America's most inspirational patriotic hymns.

WHAT A FRIEND WE HAVE
IN JESUS

"What a Friend We Have in Jesus" has long been associated with the United States of America. This is probably due in part to the fact that this country has a reputation for being the most generous nation in the world. After World War II, the United States and its people helped rebuild the very nations that attacked us. When countries—even those who were enemies of the United States—have experienced great national disasters such as earthquakes, floods, or famine, Americans have always been among the first to respond with aid. In Christian circles it may be the American missionaries who are the best known of the foreigners who go into the most remote parts of the Third World to bring help and hope.

Though many in the U.S. judge the country, its government, and its people as not coming close to the ideals set in motion by Christ, most of the world's people are still amazed by America's dynamic rush to help "the least of these." In hundreds of millions of minds, the U.S. has traditionally been viewed as a Christian country because of the compassion it has shown to those in need. So for many of those whose lives have been saved or altered by America's outreach and generosity, "What a Friend We Have in Jesus" is the song that best defines their view of this country. Yet this old hymn was not written by an American; rather, it was composed in Canada by a man who was born in Europe.

One hundred and fifty years ago, two businessmen stood on a frigid Port Hope, Ontario, street corner as snow spit from a gray sky. In the midst of that bitterly cold day, a little man carrying a saw walked by. After the two friends watched the woodcutter pass, one of them observed, "Now there is a man happy with his lot in life. I wish I could know his joy!"

"He seems to be happy, all right," the other agreed. Then he added, "I know he is a very hardworking, honest man."

"If he is such a happy worker and honest too," the first businessman responded, "then maybe I should run after him and hire him to cut some wood for me. I'm going to need some more to make it through the long winter months."

"Oh," came the laughing reply, "he would not work for you."

"And why not?" demanded the first man. "I would pay him a fair wage!"

"It's not that at all. You see, Joseph Scriven only cuts wood for people who cannot afford to pay anyone to cut it for them, or for those who cannot cut it for themselves. Scriven gives his work to people in need and takes nothing for himself."

The man who exemplified Christian charity was born in Ireland in 1819. He did not have a life so charmed that faith came easily. In fact the woodcutter with the bright smile and gentle manner had suffered more heartache and woe than would hit most families in three generations. The son of a captain in the British Royal Marines, Joseph received a university degree from London's Trinity College in 1844. A man of great faith and determination, he quickly established himself as a teacher, fell in love, and made plans to settle in his hometown. Then tragedy struck. The day before his wedding, his fiancée drowned.

Overcome with grief, Scriven left Ireland to start a new life in Canada. He taught school in Woodstock and Brantford

What a Friend we have in Jesus,
All our sins and griefs to bear!
What a privilege to carry
Everything to God in Prayer!
O what peace we often forfeit,
O what needless pain we bear,
All because we do not carry,
Everything to God in Prayer!

Have we trials and temptations?
Is there trouble anywhere?
We should never be discouraged,
Take it to the Lord in prayer.
Can we find a friend so faithful
Who will all our sorrows share?
Jesus knows our every weakness,
Take it to the Lord in prayer.

Are we weak and heavy-laden,
Cumbered with a load of care?
Precious Savior, still our refuge —
Take it to the Lord in prayer.
Do thy friends despise, forsake thee?
Take it to the Lord in prayer;
In His arms He'll take and shield thee,
Thou wilt find a solace there.

before establishing a home in Rice Lake. It was there he met and fell in love with Eliza Rice. Just weeks before she was to become Scriven's bride, she suddenly grew sick. Though the best doctors from across the area were called in, nothing they did seemed to help. In a matter of weeks, Eliza died. A shattered Scriven turned to the only thing that had anchored him during his life—his faith. Through prayer and Bible study he somehow found not just solace but a mission. The twenty-five-year-old man decided to take to heart Jesus' "Sermon on the Mount." He sold all his earthly possessions and vowed to give his life to the physically handicapped and financially destitute. It was a vow he never broke.

Ten years later Scriven received news that his mother had become very ill. The man who had taken a vow of poverty did not have the funds to go home and help care for the woman who had given him birth. Heartsick, feeling a need to reach out to her, Scriven first turned to prayer and then to words. In a letter to his mother, this friend of the friendless wrote the story of his life in three short verses he called "What a Friend We Have in Jesus." Scriven, who later said, "The Lord and I wrote the song together," shared the poem with a few acquaintances. One of them took copies to a music publisher. Within two years the little poem of inspiration had been published and coupled to a tune written by an American lawyer, Charles Converse.

"What a Friend We Have in Jesus" might have remained as obscure as Joseph Scriven if it had not been for the American evangelist Dwight L. Moody. Moody came across the song some two decades after it was written and believed it to be the most touching modern hymn he had ever heard. It was Moody, through his meetings, teachings, and books, who gave the song a national platform and probably created the impression that "What a Friend We Have in Jesus" had been written in the United States.

In the late 1800s American missionaries took the hymn to the four corners of the globe. "What a Friend We Have in Jesus" was one of the first American songs learned by many of those touched by these missionaries' work. Because of missionaries the song became so associated with the United States and its people that by the turn of the century many Eastern European immigrants sang "What a Friend" as they arrived at Ellis Island. Many of these potential Americans did not understand a single word of English, but in their hearts they believed the United States was a place where Jesus was everyone's friend.

The same thoughts and inspiration that Joseph Scriven wanted to give his sick mother in 1855, the idea that missionaries passed along in foreign lands for generations, and the hope that immigrants clung to as they arrived in the United States were adopted by millions of Christians during World War I and World War II. "What a Friend We Have in Jesus" was usually sung in American churches on the Sunday morning before a church member left for military service. This song, along with "Amazing Grace," was also the most common hymn played if that same man was lost in combat. Thus for tens of millions of Americans, "What a Friend We Have In Jesus" became the spiritual reinforcement that got them through the most trying times of their lives. In the process the hymn had somehow grown beyond the autobiographical testimony of an Irishman, whose life had seen little but trouble and sacrifice, and into an anthem whose message was universal in moments of insecurity and doubt.

Ironically, Joseph Scriven drowned in a Canadian lake in 1886. While he did realize that the poem meant only for his mother's eyes had become meaningful to others, the man with the giving spirit did not live long enough to see "What a Friend We Have in Jesus" taken to every corner of the globe. Yet Scriven, who spent fifty years cutting wood and giving all he had to "the least of these," would have surely been pleased to know that his life's message, written in a poem, has inspired so many for so long.

Name Index